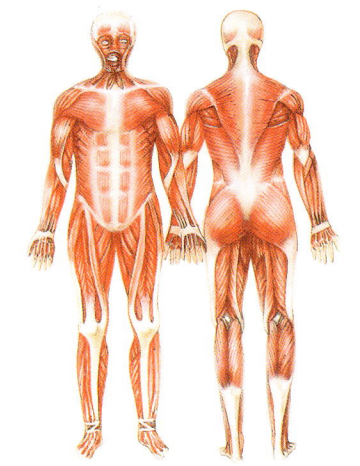

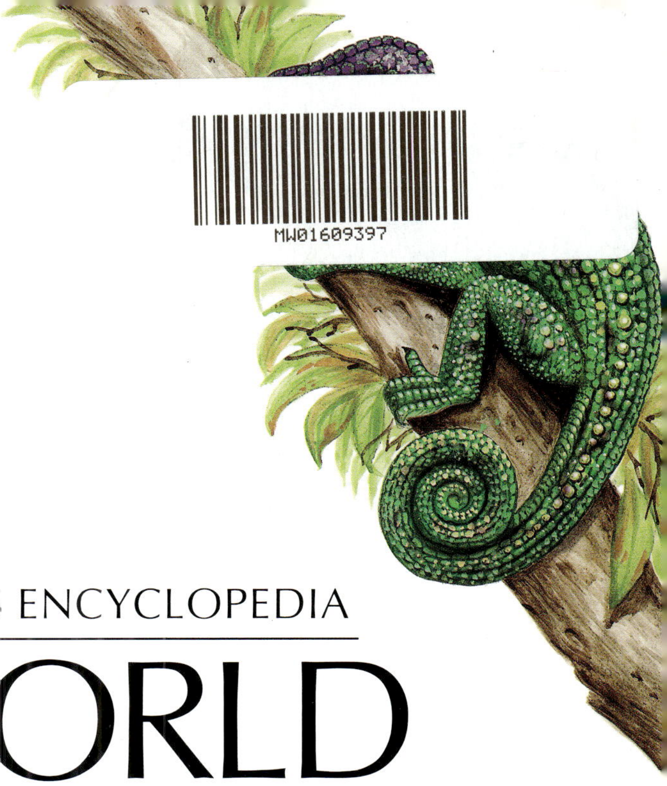

QUESTIONS & ANSWERS ENCYCLOPEDIA

OUR WORLD

QUESTIONS & ANSWERS ENCYCLOPEDIA

OUR WORLD

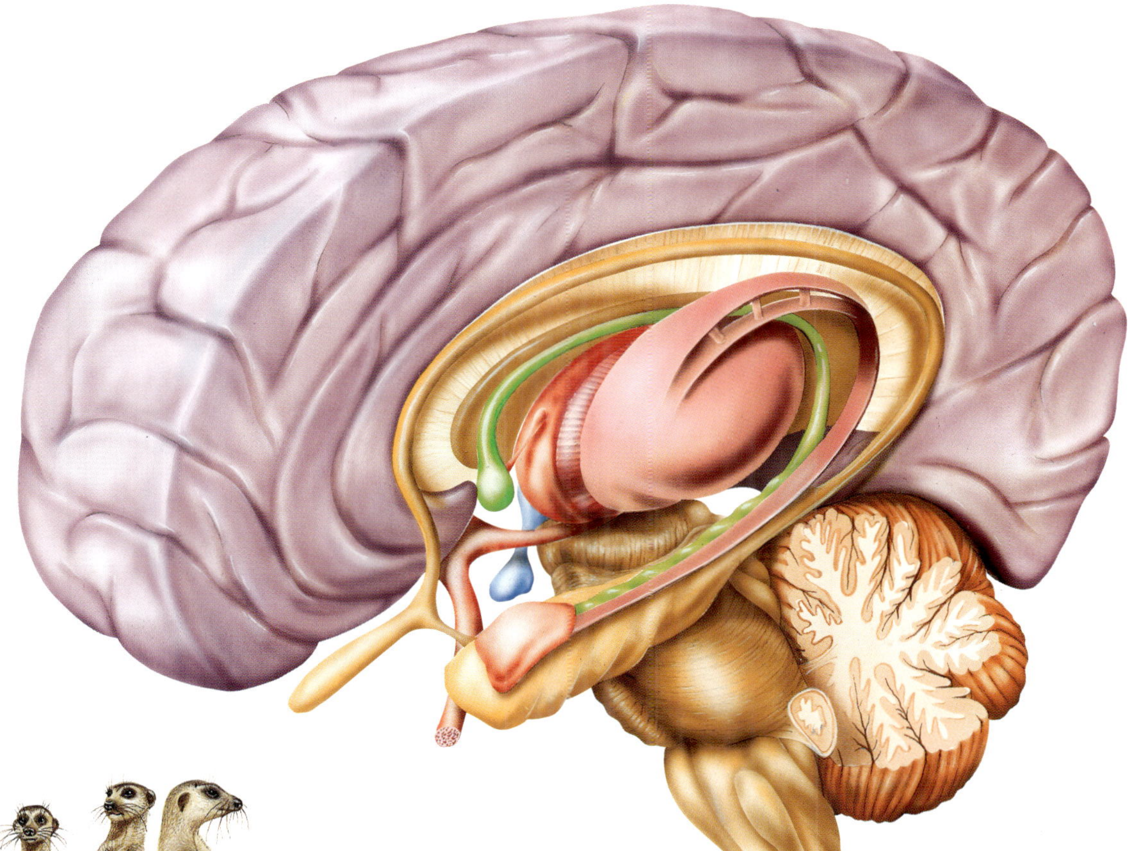

p

This is a Parragon Publishing Book
This edition published in 2003
Parragon Publishing
Queen Street House
4 Queen Street
Bath BA1 1HE, UK

Copyright © Parragon 2001

This book was created by Blackjacks Limited

ISBN 0-75259-624-1

Printed in China

Written by John Farndon, Colin Hynson, Ian James,
Jinny Johnson, Fiona Macdonald, Angela Royston,
Philip Steele, Martin Walters.

Illustrated by David Ashby, Mike Atkinson, Julian Baker,
Andrew Farmer, Rob Jakeway, John James, Roger Kent
and David McAllister.

CONTENTS

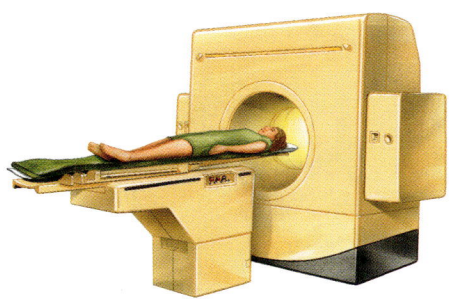

OUR
PLANET

ARCHEAN 4,600–2,500 m.y.a.

EARTH'S
FORMATION

THE GEOLOGICAL TIME SCALE

*The Earth was formed from a
cloud of gas and dust around
4,600 million years ago.*

PROTEROZOIC
2,500–590 m.y.a.

HOW IS EARTH'S HISTORY DIVIDED UP?

Scientists divide the last 590 million years of Earth's history into three main eras: the Paleozoic (a word meaning "old life") era, the Mesozoic ("middle life") era, and the Cenozoic ("new life") era. The eras are then subdivided into periods—and some periods are further divided into epochs. The first period in the Paleozoic era is the Cambrian period. All of Earth's history before the Cambrian period is called the Precambrian. Scientists divide the Precambrian into two eons: the Archean and the Proterozoic. Scientists know little about life in the Precambrian, because fossils from that time are rare.

WHAT WAS THE EARTH LIKE AFTER IT FORMED?

The Earth's surface was probably molten (hot and liquid) for many millions of years after its formation. The oldest known rocks are about 3,960 million years old.

WHEN DID LIVING THINGS FIRST APPEAR ON EARTH?

The oldest known fossils (of microscopic bacteria) are around 3,500 million years old. Primitive life forms may have first appeared on Earth about 3,850 million years ago.

WHY IS THE CAMBRIAN PERIOD IMPORTANT?

During the Precambrian, most living creatures were soft-bodied and they left few fossils. During the Cambrian period, many creatures had hard parts, which were preserved as fossils in layers of rock.

WHAT WERE THE FIRST ANIMALS WITH BACKBONES?

Jawless fishes were the first animals with backbones. They appeared during the Ordovician period. Fishes with skeletons of cartilage, such as sharks, first appeared in the Devonian period.

WHEN DID PLANTS START TO GROW ON LAND?

The first land plants appeared in the Silurian period. Plants produced oxygen and provided food for the first land animals, amphibians. Amphibians first appeared in the Devonian period.

WHEN DID MAMMALS FIRST APPEAR?

Mammals lived on Earth from at least the start of the Jurassic period. But they did not become common until after the extinction of the dinosaurs.

WHEN DID PEOPLE FIRST LIVE ON EARTH?

Hominids (ape-like creatures that walked upright) first appeared on Earth more than four million years ago. But modern humans appeared only around 100,000 years ago.

The Archean and Proterozoic eons together occupied 87% of Earth history.

WHY DID THE DINOSAURS BECOME EXTINCT?

The dinosaurs first appeared on Earth during the Triassic period. They became the dominant animals during the Jurassic period, but at the end of the Cretaceous period, 65 million years ago, they became extinct. Scientists still argue about why they disappeared. But many experts now believe that around 65 million years ago an enormous asteroid struck the Earth. The impact threw up a huge cloud of dust, which blocked out the sunlight for a long time. Land plants died and so the dinosaurs starved to death.

The last 590 million years of Earth history are divided into eras and periods. "M.y.a." on the diagram means "millions of years ago."

590 m.y.a.

PRECAMBRIAN

505 m.y.a.

CAMBRIAN PERIOD

438 m.y.a.

408 m.y.a.

ORDOVICIAN PERIOD

SILURIAN PERIOD

360 m.y.a.

DEVONIAN PERIOD

286 m.y.a.

CARBONIFEROUS PERIOD

248 m.y.a.

PALEOZOIC ERA

PERMIAN PERIOD

213 m.y.a.

TRIASSIC PERIOD

144 m.y.a.

JURASSIC PERIOD

MESOZOIC ERA

CRETACEOUS PERIOD

65 m.y.a.

TERTIARY PERIOD

CENOZOIC ERA

2 m.y.a.

QUATERNARY PERIOD

Today

WHAT IS THE BIGGEST CONTINENT?

Asia covers an area of 16,992,000 sq miles the other continents, in order of size, are Africa (11,678,000 sq miles), North America (9,351,000 sq miles), South America (6,885,000 sq miles), Antarctica (5,400,400 sq miles), Europe (4,032,000 sq miles), and Australia (2,978,000 sq miles).

HOW MUCH OF THE WORLD IS COVERED BY LAND?

Land covers about 57,300,000 sq miles, or 29% of the world's surface. Water covers the remaining 71%.

WHAT IS THE WORLD'S LARGEST ISLAND?

Greenland covers about 840,000 sq miles. Geographers regard Australia as a continent and not as an island.

WHAT IS THE WORLD'S LARGEST HIGH PLATEAU?

The wind-swept Tibetan Plateau in China covers about 715,000 sq miles.

WHERE IS THE WORLD'S LOWEST POINT ON LAND?

The shoreline of the Dead Sea, between Israel and Jordan, is 1,312 feet below the sea level of the nearby Mediterranean Sea.

WHAT IS THE WORLD'S HIGHEST PEAK?

Mount Everest on Nepal's border with China reaches 29,029 feet above sea level. Measured from its base on the sea floor, Mauna Kea, Hawaii, is 33,474 feet high. But only 13,796 feet appear above sea level.

WHERE DO MOST PEOPLE LIVE?

The continent with the largest population is Asia, which has more than 3,000 million people. Europe ranks second in world population, followed by Africa, North America, South America, and Australia. The continent of Antarctica has no permanent population at all.

WHAT IS THE LARGEST INLAND BODY OF WATER OR LAKE?

The salty Caspian Sea, which lies partly in Europe and partly in Asia, has an area of about 143,390 sq miles. The largest freshwater lake is Lake Superior, one of the Great Lakes of North America. Lake Superior has an area of 31,796 sq miles.

WHAT IS THE WORLD'S LONGEST RIVER?

The Nile in north-eastern Africa is 4,112 miles long. The second longest river, the Amazon in South America, discharges 60 times more water than the Nile.

WHICH IS THE DEEPEST LAKE?

Lake Baikal, in Siberia, eastern Russia, is the world's deepest lake. The deepest spot measured so far is 5,371 feet.

WHAT IS THE WORLD'S LARGEST RIVER BASIN?

The Amazon river basin in South America covers about 2,720,000 sq miles. The Madeira River, which flows into the Amazon, is the world's longest tributary, at 2,100 miles.

WHAT IS THE WORLD'S LARGEST DESERT?

The Sahara in North Africa covers an area of about 3,579,000 sq miles. This is nearly as big as the United States.

When volcanoes erupt, they may hurl rocks and ash into the air, and lava may flow down slopes.

WHAT MAKES VOLCANOES ERUPT?

Volcanoes erupt when hot molten rock from deep down in the Earth's mantle rises through the Earth's hard outer layers and reaches the surface. The molten rock is called magma, but when it reaches the surface, it is called lava. Most volcanoes occur near the edges of plates. Many rise along the ocean ridges where magma rushes up to fill the gaps formed as plates move apart. Other volcanoes get their magma from the plates that are melted as they are pulled beneath other plates.

WHAT ARE VOLCANOES MADE OF?

Some volcanoes are cone-shaped and made of volcanic ash or cinders. Dome-shaped shield volcanoes are made of hardened lava. Intermediate volcanoes contain layers of both ash and lava.

Magma reaches the surface through vents, which are holes in the ground.

Lava may burst from a central vent or through side vents.

Lava flows burn everything in their paths.

DO ALL VOLCANOES ERUPT IN THE SAME WAY?

No, they don't. Volcanoes can explode upward or sideways, or erupt "quietly." Trapped inside the magma in explosive volcanoes are lots of gases and water vapor. These gases shatter the magma and hurl columns of volcanic ash and fine volcanic dust into the air. Fragments of shattered magma are called pyroclasts. Sometimes, clouds of ash and hot gases are shot sideways out of volcanoes. They pour downhill at great speeds destroying everything in their paths. In "quietly" erupting volcanoes the magma emerges on the surface as runny lava and flows downhill.

KINDS OF VOLCANOES

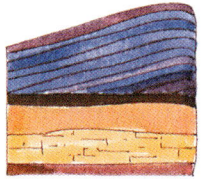

SHIELD VOLCANO
Some volcanoes, shaped like upturned shields, are formed by "quiet eruptions," in which long streams of very fluid lava are emitted.

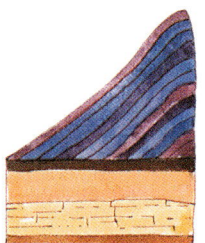

EXPLOSIVE VOLCANO
Explosive eruptions occur when the magma is thick and contains explosive gases. Explosive volcanoes are made of ash and cinders and are steep-sided.

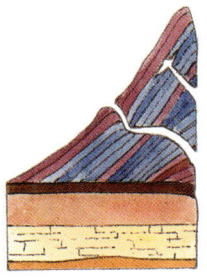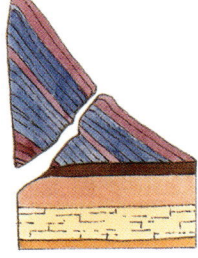

INTERMEDIATE VOLCANO
Intermediate volcanoes are cone-shaped. They are composed of alternating layers of ash and hardened lava.

Some volcanoes shoot fountains of hot melted rock into the air.

WHAT IS AN EXTINCT VOLCANO?

Volcanoes that have not erupted in historic times are said to be extinct. This means that they are not expected to erupt ever again.

WHAT ARE "HOT SPOTS?"

Some volcanoes lie far from plate edges. They form over "hot spots"—areas of great heat in the Earth's mantle. Hawaii in the Pacific Ocean is over a hot spot.

WHAT IS A DORMANT VOLCANO?

Some volcanoes erupt continuously for long periods. But other active volcanoes erupt only now and then. When they are not erupting, they are said to be dormant, or sleeping.

When lava and volcanic ash harden, they slowly break down to form soil.

Frost action affects high mountain slopes, where water freezes at night.

HOW DOES WEATHERING HELP TO SHAPE THE LAND?

Weathering is the breakdown and decay of rocks on the Earth's surface. The wearing away of the rock limestone is an example of chemical weathering. Limestone consists mostly of the chemical calcium carbonate. This chemical reacts with rainwater containing carbon dioxide, which it has dissolved from the air. The rainwater is a weak acid that slowly dissolves the limestone. The rainwater opens up cracks in the surface, wearing out holes that eventually lead down to a maze of huge caves linked by tunnels.

Surface water flows into layers of limestone and hollows out caves.

WHAT IS BIOLOGICAL WEATHERING?

Biological weathering includes the splitting apart of rocks by tree roots, the breaking up of rocks by burrowing animals, and the work of bacteria, which also helps to weather rocks.

WHAT ARE POT-HOLERS?

Pot-holes, or swallow holes, are holes in the ground where people called pot-holers can climb down to explore limestone caves. Pot-holers may face danger when sudden rains raise the water level in caves.

Weathering is rapid on sloping land, where worn rocks tumble downhill.

Worn rocks pile up in heaps called scree or talus.

DOES WATER REACT CHEMICALLY WITH OTHER ROCKS?

Water dissolves rock salt. It also reacts with some types of the hard rock granite, turning minerals in the rock into a clay called kaolin.

WHAT IS GROUND WATER?

Ground water is water that seeps slowly through rocks, such as sandstones and limestones. The top level of the water in the rocks is called the water table. Wells are dug down to the water table.

HOW QUICKLY IS THE LAND WORN AWAY?

Scientists have worked out that an average of 1⅜ inch is worn away from land areas every 1,000 years. This sounds slow but, over millions of years, mountains are worn down to make plains.

CAN THE SUN'S HEAT CAUSE MECHANICAL WEATHERING?

In hot, dry regions, rocks are heated by the Sun, but they cool at night. These changes crack rock surfaces, which peel away like the layers of an onion.

WHAT ARE STALAGMITES?

Stalagmites are the opposite of stalactites. They are columns of calcium carbonate deposited by dripping water. But stalagmites grow upward from the floors of caves.

WHAT ARE SPRINGS?

Springs occur when ground water flows on to the surface. Springs are the sources of many rivers. Hot springs occur in volcanic areas, where the ground water is heated by magma.

The roots of trees can split rock apart.

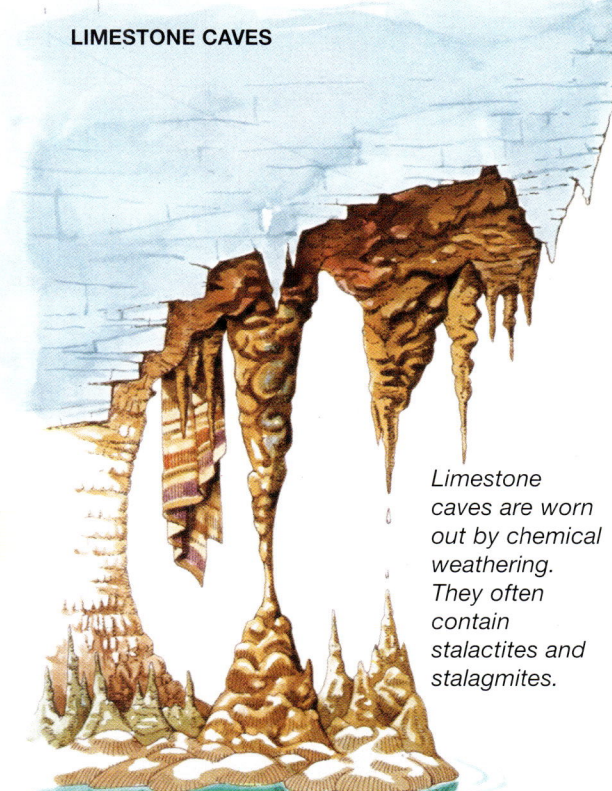

Limestone caves are worn out by chemical weathering. They often contain stalactites and stalagmites.

WHAT ARE STALACTITES?

Water containing a lot of calcium carbonate drips down from the ceilings of limestone caves. The water gradually deposits calcium carbonate to form hanging, icicle-like structures called stalactites.

HOW DOES THE ACTION OF FROST BREAK UP ROCKS?

At night in the mountains, people may hear sounds like gunshots. These sounds are made by rocks being split apart by frost action. Frost action, an example of mechanical weathering, occurs when water in cracks in rocks freezes and turns into ice. Ice takes up nearly one-tenth as much space again as water, and so it exerts pressure, widening the cracks until they split apart. On steep slopes, shattered rocks tumble downhill and pile up in heaps, called scree or talus.

Ground water flows out of limestone caves to form the source of a river.

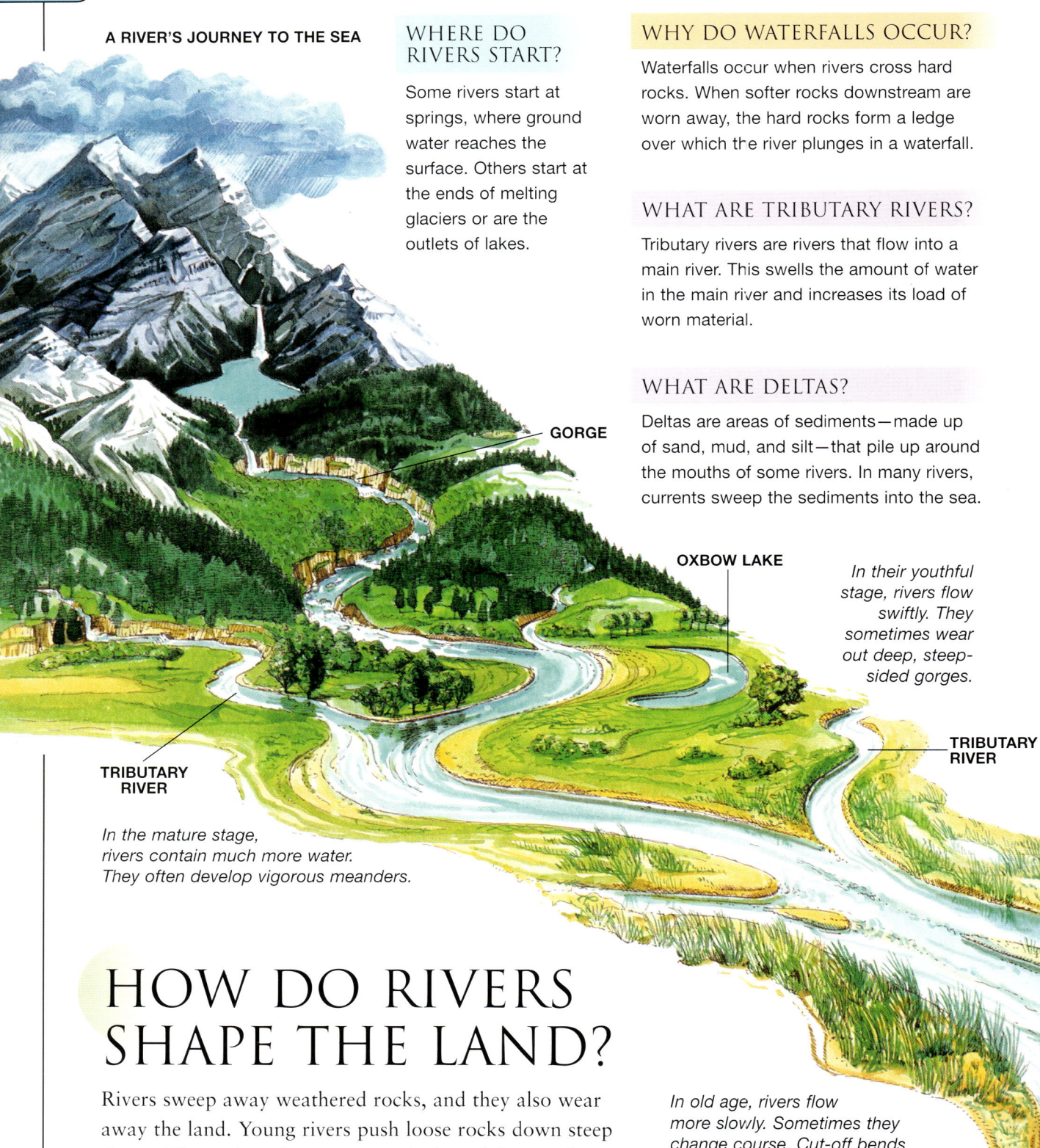

A RIVER'S JOURNEY TO THE SEA

WHERE DO RIVERS START?

Some rivers start at springs, where ground water reaches the surface. Others start at the ends of melting glaciers or are the outlets of lakes.

WHY DO WATERFALLS OCCUR?

Waterfalls occur when rivers cross hard rocks. When softer rocks downstream are worn away, the hard rocks form a ledge over which the river plunges in a waterfall.

WHAT ARE TRIBUTARY RIVERS?

Tributary rivers are rivers that flow into a main river. This swells the amount of water in the main river and increases its load of worn material.

WHAT ARE DELTAS?

Deltas are areas of sediments—made up of sand, mud, and silt—that pile up around the mouths of some rivers. In many rivers, currents sweep the sediments into the sea.

GORGE

OXBOW LAKE

In their youthful stage, rivers flow swiftly. They sometimes wear out deep, steep-sided gorges.

TRIBUTARY RIVER

TRIBUTARY RIVER

In the mature stage, rivers contain much more water. They often develop vigorous meanders.

HOW DO RIVERS SHAPE THE LAND?

Rivers sweep away weathered rocks, and they also wear away the land. Young rivers push loose rocks down steep slopes. The rocks rub against riverbeds and deepen their valleys. The rocks rub against each other and break down into finer and finer pieces. Mature rivers flow down gentler slopes. They develop bends called meanders and they continue to wear away land. In old age rivers move slowly across nearly flat plains, carrying huge loads of sand, silt, and mud toward the sea.

In old age, rivers flow more slowly. Sometimes they change course. Cut-off bends become oxbow lakes.

When heavy rains swell old-age rivers, they may overflow their banks and cause floods.

Waves hollow out caves in rocky headlands. Blow-holes form above the caves.

When two caves in a headland meet, a natural arch occurs.

When a natural arch collapses, the tip of the headland becomes an isolated stack.

CAN SEA WAVES SHAPE COASTS?

Large storm waves batter the shore. The waves pick up sand and pebbles, hurling them at cliffs. This hollows out the bottom layers of the cliff until the top collapses and the cliff retreats. Waves hollow out bays in soft rocks, leaving hard rocks jutting into the sea as headlands. Waves then attack the headlands from both sides, wearing out caves. When two caves meet, a natural arch is formed. When the arch collapses, all that remains is an isolated rock, called a stack.

WHAT ARE SPITS?

Waves and currents transport sediments along coasts. In places where the coasts change direction, the worn sand and pebbles pile up in narrow ridges called spits.

WHAT IS A BAYMOUTH BAR?

Some spits join one headland to another. They are called baymouth bars, because they cut off bays from the sea, turning them into lagoons.

DOES THE SEA WEAR AWAY THE LAND?

Waves wear away soft rocks to form bays, while harder rocks on either side form headlands. Parts of the coast of Northeast England have been worn back by up to 3 miles since the days when the Romans ruled the area.

HOW CAN PEOPLE SLOW DOWN WAVE EROSION?

Along the beaches at many coastal resorts, walls are built at right angles to the shore. These walls, called groynes, slow down the movement of sand on the beaches by waves and sea currents.

Mud carried by a river is often dumped near the river's mouth to form large mud flats. At high tide the sea often covers these areas.

HOW DOES ICE SHAPE THE LAND?

Snow falls on mountains. At the higher levels, the snow piles up year by year.

In cold mountain areas, snow piles up in hollows. Gradually, the snow becomes compacted into ice. Eventually, the ice spills out of the hollows and starts to move downhill to form a glacier. Glaciers are like conveyor belts. On the tops of glaciers are rocks shattered by frost action that have tumbled downhill. Other rocks are frozen into the sides and bottoms of glaciers. They give glaciers the power to wear away rocks and deepen the valleys through which they flow. Ice-worn valleys are U-shaped, with steep sides and flat bottoms. This distinguishes them from V-shaped river valleys.

WHAT ARE THE WORLD'S LARGEST BODIES OF ICE?

The largest bodies of ice are the ice sheets of Antarctica and Greenland. Smaller ice caps occur in the Arctic, while mountain glaciers are found around the world.

A VALLEY GLACIER

Snow in mountain basins, called cirques, becomes compressed into glacier ice.

HOW MUCH OF THE WORLD IS COVERED BY ICE?

Ice covers about 11% of the world's land area. But during the last Ice Age, it spread over much of northern North America and Europe. The same ice sheet reached what is now New York City in America, and covered London in England.

The ice spills downhill to form rivers of ice called glaciers. The glaciers carry much worn rock, called moraine.

WHAT ARE ERRATICS?

Erratics are boulders made of a rock that is different from the rocks on which they rest. They were transported to their present positions by moving ice.

WHAT ARE FIORDS?

Fiords are deep, steep-sided valleys that wind inland along coasts. They were once river valleys that were deepened by glaciers during the last Ice Age.

THE WORLD MAP DURING THE ICE AGE

WHAT IS AN ICE AGE?

During ice ages, average temperatures fall and ice sheets spread over large areas that were once ice-free. Several ice ages have occurred in Earth's history.

Ice covered much of northern North America, Europe, and Asia during the Ice Age.

WHEN DID THE LAST ICE AGE TAKE PLACE?

The last Ice Age began about two million years ago and ended 10,000 years ago. The Ice Age included warm periods and long periods of bitter cold.

HOW CAN WE TELL THAT AN AREA WAS ONCE COVERED BY ICE?

Certain features in the landscape were made by ice during the ice ages. Mountain areas contain deep, steep-sided valleys that were worn out by glaciers. Armchair-shaped basins where glacier ice once formed are called cirques. Knife-edged ridges between cirques are called arêtes, while peaks called horns were carved when three or more cirques formed back-to-back. Boulders and other material carried by ice is called moraine. Moraine ridges show that ice sheets once reached that area.

At the end of the glacier, the ice melts, creating streams that sweep away the glacier's rocky load.

WHAT ARE THE MAIN TYPES OF DESERT SCENERY?

Arabic words are used for desert scenery. "Erg" is the name for sandy desert, "reg" is land covered with gravel and pebbles, and "hammada" is the word for areas of bare rock.

Human misuse of the land near deserts, caused by cutting down trees and overgrazing grasslands, may turn fertile land into desert. This is called desertification. Natural climate changes may also create deserts. This happened in the Sahara around 7,000 years ago.

MUSHROOM ROCKS

Wind-blown sand erodes the bottoms of rocks, wearing them to a narrow stem.

HOW DOES WIND-BLOWN SAND SHAPE SCENERY?

In deserts, wind-blown sand is important in shaping the scenery. Winds lift grains of sand, which are then blown and bounced forward. Sand grains are heavy and seldom rise over 6 feet above ground level. But, at low levels, wind-blown sand acts like the sand-blasters used to clean dirty city buildings. It also polishes rocks, hollows out caves in cliffs, and undercuts boulders. Boulders whose bases have been worn by wind-blown sand are top-heavy and mushroom-shaped, perched on a narrow stem.

DESERT SCENERY

Oases are places in deserts where water comes to the surface or where people can obtain water from wells.

Large areas of desert are covered with gravel and pebbles. These areas are called "reg."

Wind-blown sand is responsible for carving top-heavy mushroom rocks that stand on thin stems.

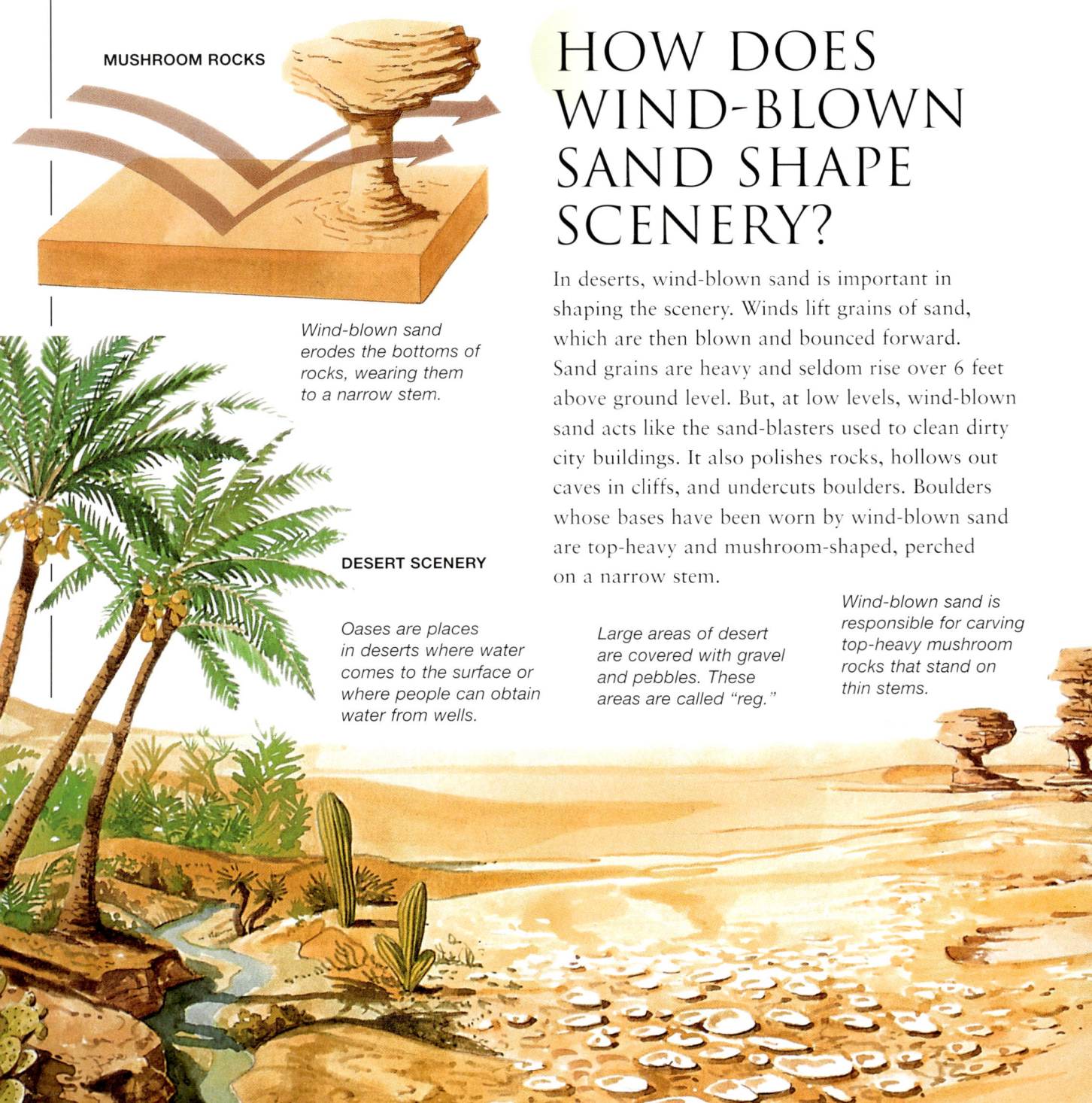

HOW ARE SAND DUNES FORMED?

Crescent-shaped dunes form in sandy deserts where wind directions are constant.

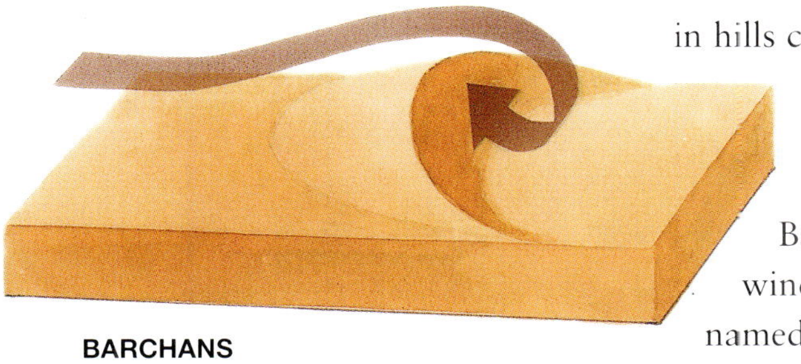

BARCHANS

The wind blowing across desert sands piles the sand up in hills called dunes. Where the wind directions keep changing, the dunes have no particular shape. But when they blow mainly from one direction, crescent-shaped dunes called barchans often form. Barchans may occur singly or in clusters. When winds drive sand dunes forward they form seif dunes, named after an Arabic word meaning sword. Sometimes, advancing dunes bury farmland. To stop their advance, people plant trees and grasses to anchor the sand.

WHY DO PEOPLE IN DESERTS WEAR HEAVY CLOTHES?

Deserts are often cold at night and heavy clothes keep people warm. Long cloaks and headdresses also help to keep out stinging wind-blown sand and dust and prevent sunburn.

WHAT ARE DUST STORMS?

Desert winds sweep fine dust high into the air during choking dust storms. Wind from the Sahara in North Africa is often blown over southern Europe, carrying the pinkish dust with it.

WHAT ARE WADIS?

Wadis are dry waterways in deserts. Travelers sometimes shelter in them at night. But a freak storm can soon fill them with water and people sleeping in the wadis are in danger of being drowned.

WHAT ARE OASES?

Oases are places in deserts that have water supplies. Some oases have wells tapping ground water. Sometimes, the water bubbles up to the surface in a spring.

About one-fifth of the world's deserts are covered in sand (erg). There are also large areas of bare rock (hammada).

JAGGED ICEBERGS

WHY ARE ICEBERGS DANGEROUS TO SHIPPING?

Icebergs are huge chunks of ice that break off from glaciers. They float in the sea with nine-tenths of their bulk submerged, which makes them extremely dangerous to shipping. Icebergs from Greenland have sunk ships off the coasts of North America.

High jagged icebergs break away from valley glaciers.

WHAT IS IT LIKE AROUND THE NORTH POLE?

It is bitterly cold. The North Pole lies in the middle of the Arctic Ocean, which is surrounded by northern North America, Asia, and Europe. Sea ice covers much of the ocean for most of the year. In spring, the sea ice is around 9 feet thick in mid-ocean and explorers can walk across it. The Arctic Ocean contains several islands, including Greenland, the world's largest. A huge ice sheet, the world's second largest, covers more than four-fifths of Greenland.

IS THE ICE AROUND THE POLES MELTING?

In parts of Antarctica, the ice shelves began to melt in the 1990s. Some people think this shows that the world is getting warmer because of pollution.

HOW THICK IS THE ICE IN ANTARCTICA?

The South Pole lies in the cold and windy continent of Antarctica, which is larger than either Europe or Australia. Ice and snow cover 98% of Antarctica, although some coastal areas and high peaks are ice-free. The Antarctic ice sheet is the world's largest, and contains about seven-tenths of the world's fresh water. In places, the ice is up to 3 miles thick. The world's record lowest temperature, −128.6°F, was recorded at the Vostok research station in 1983.

WHAT ANIMALS LIVE IN POLAR REGIONS?

Penguins are the best known animals of Antarctica. Polar bears, caribou, musk oxen, and reindeer are large animals that live in the Arctic region.

ICEBERGS IN THE OCEANS

The bulk of the ice in icebergs is hidden beneath the waves.

Icebergs contain worn rocks that have been eroded from the land.

Icebergs melt as they float away from polar regions and the climate becomes warmer.

As icebergs melt, the rocks in the ice sink down and settle on the ocean bed.

WHERE ARE THE POLES?

The Earth is always spinning on its axis, giving us day and night. The points at the ends of this axis are the North and South geographic poles.

WHAT ARE MAGNETIC POLES?

The Earth is like a giant magnet, with two magnetic poles. They lie near the geographic poles, though their positions change from time to time.

Flat-topped icebergs form off the coast of Antarctica.

WHAT ARE ICE SHELVES?

Ice shelves are large blocks of ice joined to Antarctica's ice sheet but which jut out over the sea. When chunks break away, they form flat, table-topped icebergs. Some of them are huge. One covered an area about the size of Belgium.

IS THERE A LAKE UNDER ANTARCTICA?

Scientists have found a lake, about the size of Lake Ontario in North America, hidden under Antarctica. It may contain creatures that lived on Earth millions of years ago.

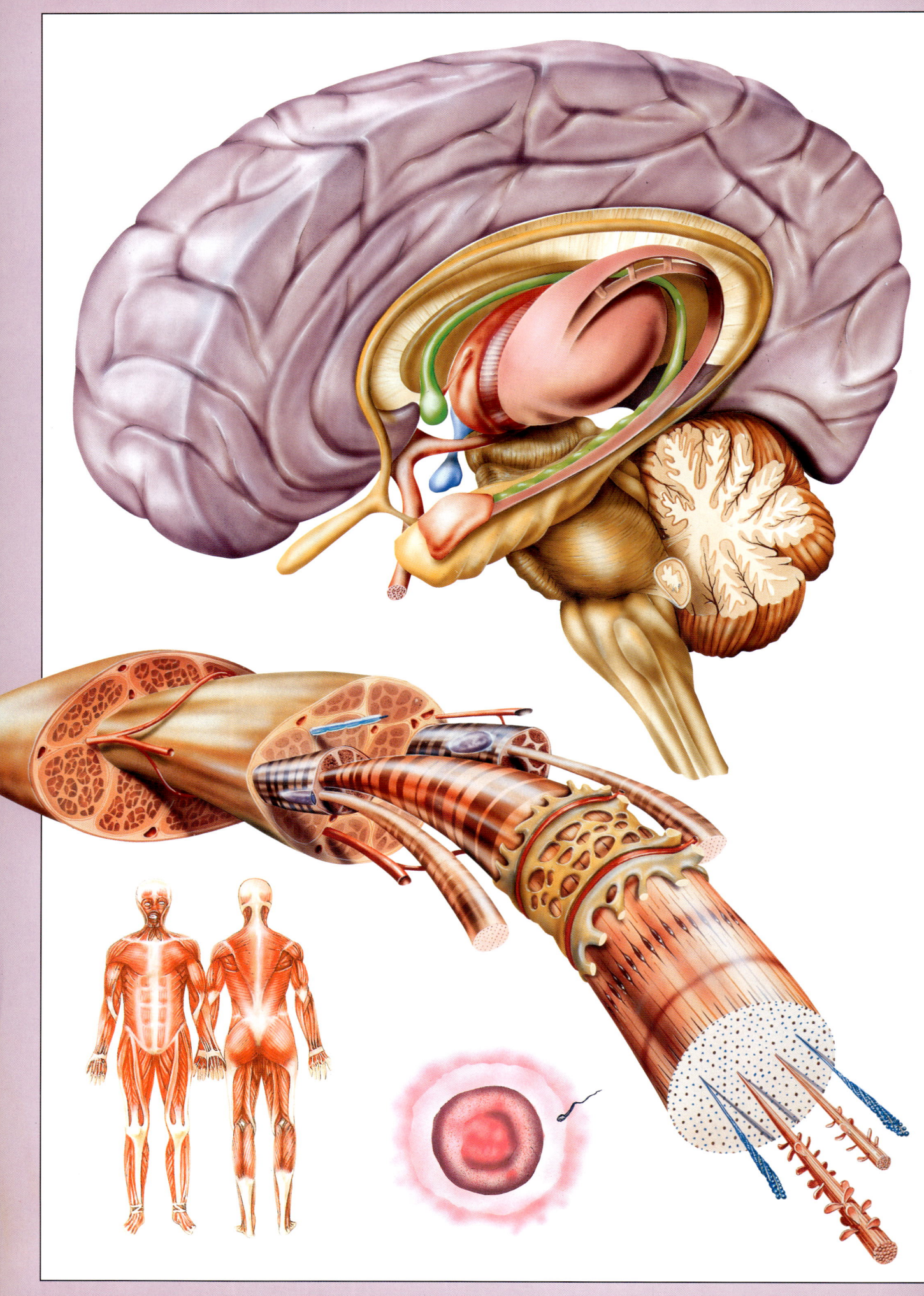

SECTION TWO

OUR BODY

WHY DO BODIES NEED BONES?

Bones provide a strong framework that supports the rest of the body. Without bones, you would flop on the floor like an octopus. Some of the bones form a suit of internal armor, which protects the brain, the lungs, the heart, and other vital organs. All the bones together are called the skeleton. You can move and bend different parts of the body because the bones meet at joints.

HOW MANY BONES DO YOU HAVE?

As a baby you had over 300 bones, but, as you grow, some bones join together. When you are an adult, you will have about 206 bones in total.

WHAT IS A VERTEBRA?

A vertebra is a knobbly bone in your spine. The 26 vertebrae fit together to make a strong pillar, the spine, which carries much of your weight. At the same time the vertebrae allow your back to bend and twist.

WHICH IS THE SMALLEST BONE?

The smallest bone is called the stirrup and is no bigger than a grain of rice. It is deep inside your ear and its job is to pass on sounds from the outer and middle ear to the inner ear.

WHICH IS THE LONGEST BONE?

The thigh bone in the upper part of your leg is the longest bone in your body. It accounts for more than a quarter of an adult's height.

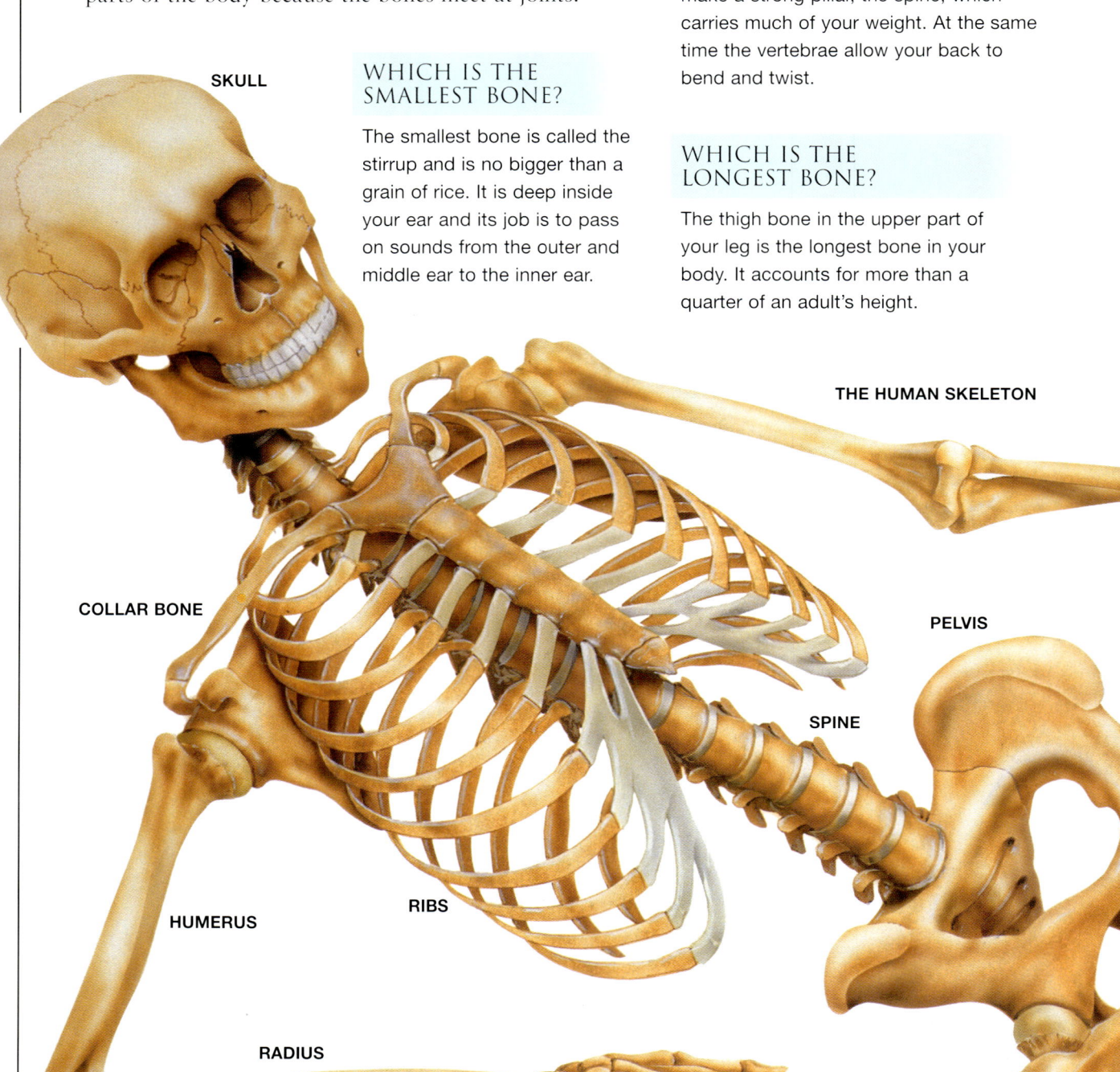

SKULL

THE HUMAN SKELETON

COLLAR BONE

PELVIS

SPINE

HUMERUS

RIBS

RADIUS

ULNA

WHAT'S INSIDE A BONE?

Inside a bone is a criss-cross honeycomb of lighter bone. Blood vessels weave in and out of the bone, keeping the cells alive. At the center of some bones is a core of bone marrow.

INSIDE A BONE

OUTER COMPACT BONE

BLOOD VESSEL

SOFTER SPONGY BONE

RED MARROW JELLY

WHY DO JOINTS NOT SQUEAK?

Joints are cushioned by soft, squashy cartilage. Many joints also contain a fluid—called synovial fluid—that works like oil to keep them moving smoothly and painlessly.

WHAT ARE LIGAMENTS?

Ligaments are strong, bendy straps that hold together the bones in a joint. Nearly all the body's joints have several ligaments.

BALL AND SOCKET JOINT

The shoulder and hip have this joint.

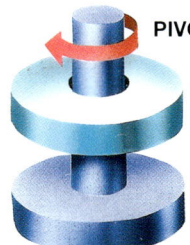

PIVOT JOINT

The pivot joint is found in the neck.

SADDLE JOINT

This joint is found at the base of the thumb.

HINGE JOINT

A joint that works like a hinge is found at the knee and elbow, and in the fingers and toes.

WHAT IS A JOINT?

Where two bones meet, their ends are shaped to make different kinds of joint. Each kind of joint makes a strong connection and allows a particular kind of movement. For example, the knee is a hinge joint that lets the lower leg move only back and forward. The hip is a ball and socket joint that allows you to move your thigh around in a circle. The saddle joint at the base of the thumb also gives a good range of movement.

FINGER BONES

PATELLA (KNEE CAP)

FEMUR (THIGH)

WHICH JOINT MOVES THE MOST?

The shoulder joint is a ball and socket joint and it allows the greatest amount of movement in all directions.

WHICH JOINTS MOVE THE LEAST?

Your skull is made up of more than 20 bones fused together in joints that allow no movement at all. These are called suture joints.

FIBULA

TIBIA (SHIN)

TOE BONES

CALCANEUS (HEEL BONE)

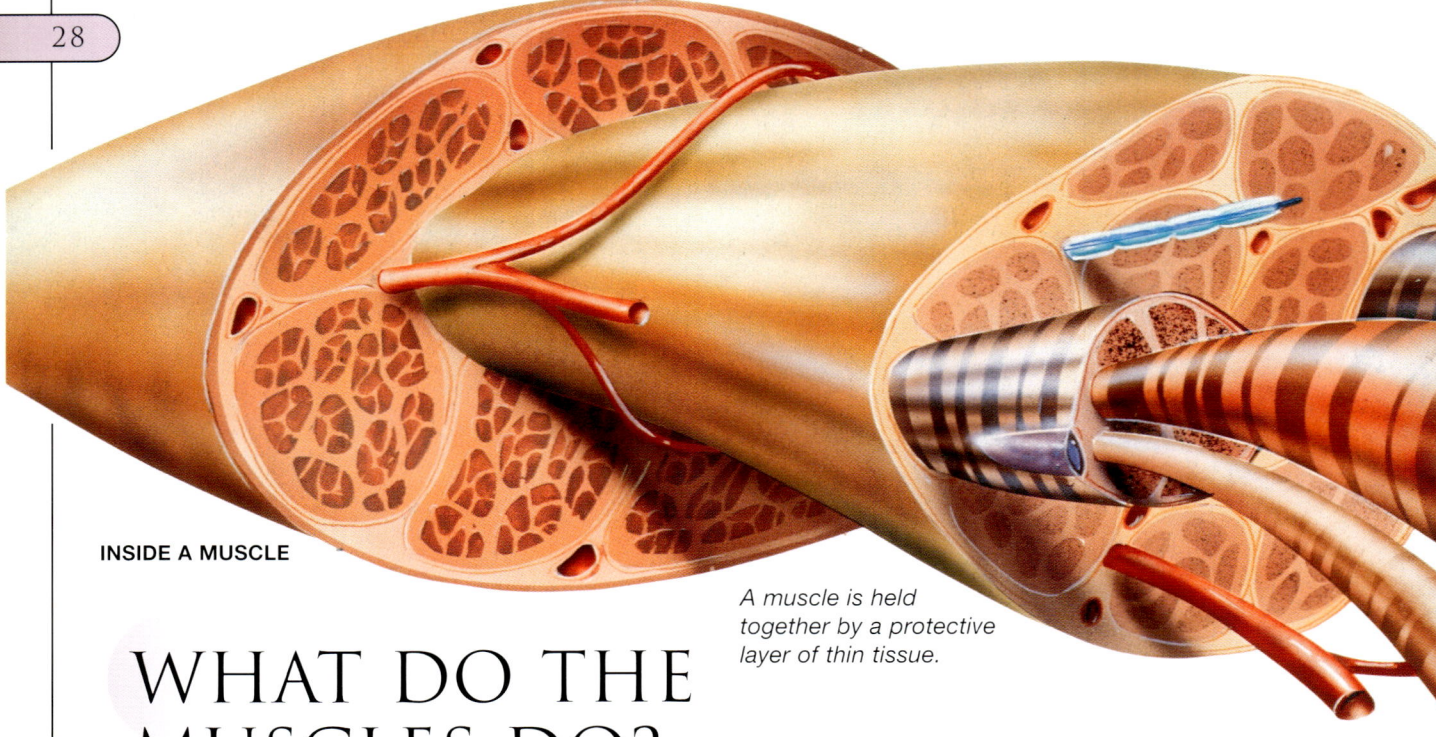

INSIDE A MUSCLE

A muscle is held together by a protective layer of thin tissue.

WHAT DO THE MUSCLES DO?

Muscles make parts of your body move. The skeleton is covered with muscles that move your bones and give your body its shape. Muscles in the face move your cheeks, eyebrows, nose, mouth, tongue, and lower jaw. A different kind of muscle works in the oesophagus (food pipe), stomach, and intestines to move food through your body. The heart is a third type of muscle—it never stops beating to move blood around your body.

THE BODY'S MUSCLES

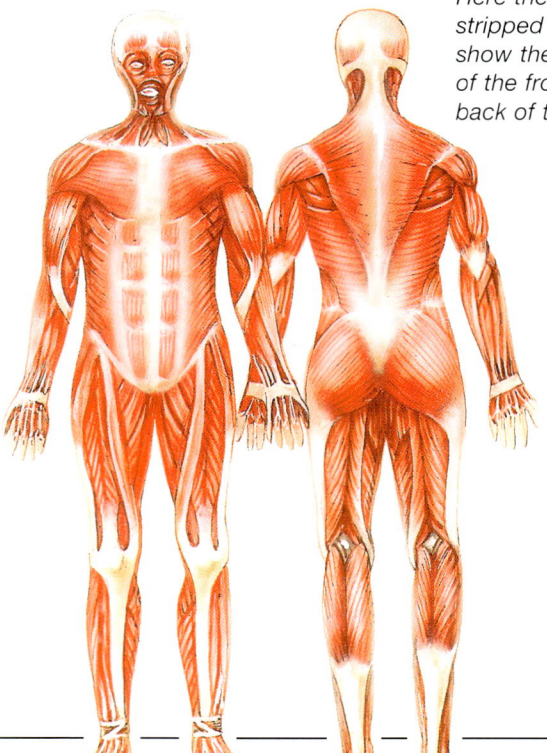

Here the skin is stripped away to show the muscles of the front and back of the body.

WHY DOES EXERCISE MAKE MUSCLES STRONGER?

A muscle is made of bundles of fibers that contract when you use the muscle. The more you use the muscle, the thicker the fibers become. They contract more effectively, which means the muscle is stronger.

HOW DO MUSCLES WORK?

Muscles work by contracting. This makes them shorter and thicker so that they pull on whatever bone or other part of the body they are attached to, thereby making it move.

WHAT IS A TENDON?

A tendon is like a tough rope that joins a muscle to a bone. If you bend and straighten your fingers, you can feel the tendons in the back of your hand. The body's strongest tendon is the Achilles tendon, which you can feel above your heel.

WHICH IS THE BIGGEST MUSCLE?

The biggest muscle is the gluteus maximus in the buttock. You use it to straighten your leg when you stand up and it makes a comfortable cushion when you sit down.

WHY DO MUSCLES WORK IN PAIRS?

Muscles cannot push—they can only pull—and so you need two sets of muscles for many actions. For example, the biceps in your upper arm bends your elbow and you can feel it tighten when you clench your arm. To straighten the elbow again, you have to relax the biceps and tighten the triceps, which is the muscle at the back of your upper arm. In the same way, one set of muscles lifts the leg and another set of muscles straightens it.

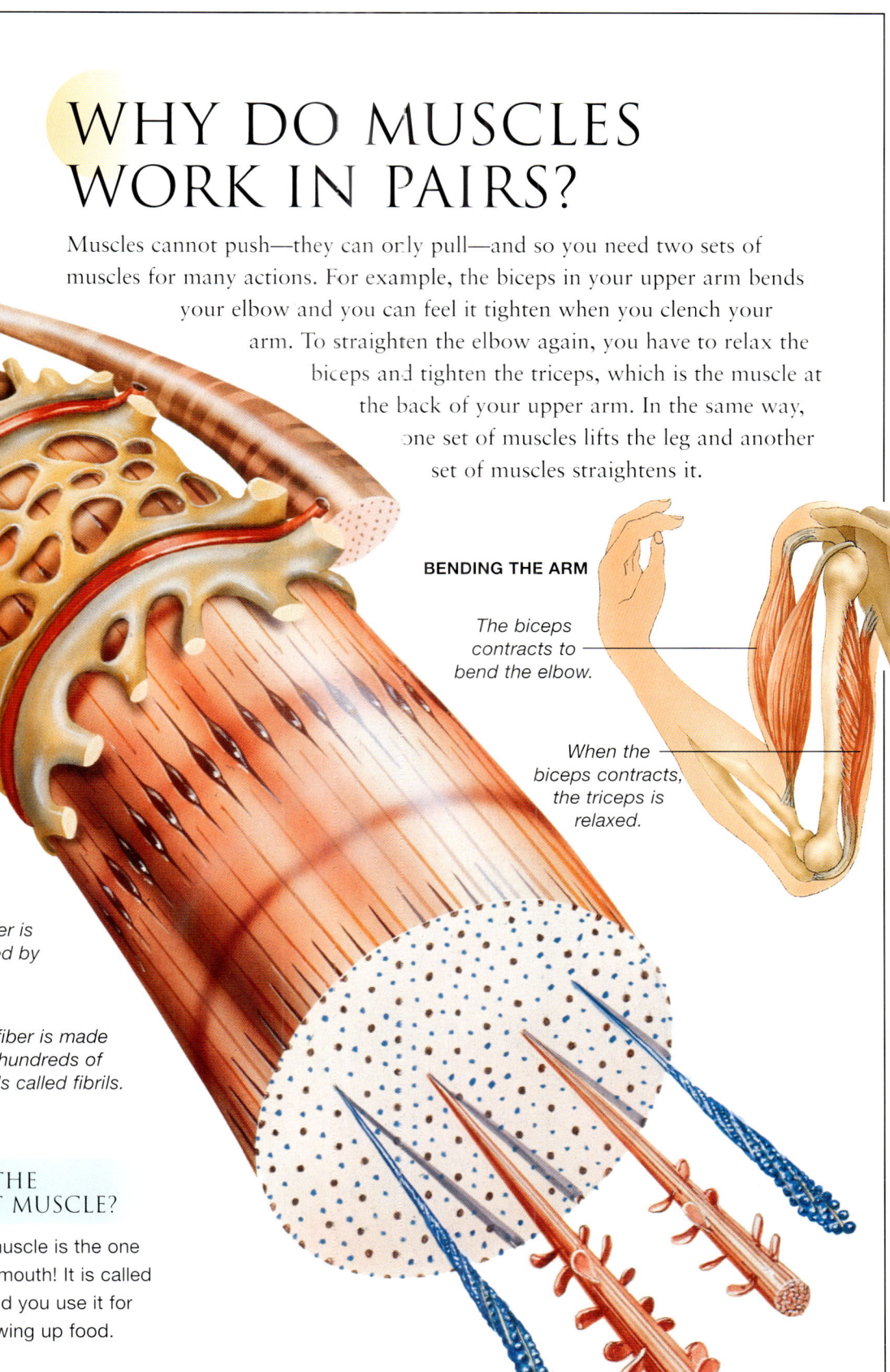

BENDING THE ARM

The biceps contracts to bend the elbow.

When the biceps contracts, the triceps is relaxed.

A muscle is made up of many bundles of fibers.

Each fiber is controlled by a nerve.

Each fiber is made up of hundreds of strands called fibrils.

WHICH IS THE STRONGEST MUSCLE?

The strongest muscle is the one that shuts your mouth! It is called the masseter and you use it for talking and chewing up food.

HOW MANY MUSCLES ARE THERE?

You have about 650 muscles that work together. Most actions—including walking, swimming, and smiling—involve dozens of muscles. Even frowning uses 40 different muscles, but smiling is less energetic—it uses only 15.

Muscle fibers are so small that ¼ square inch would contain a million of them.

HOW BIG IS THE HEART?

The heart is about the same size as your clenched fist. It lies nearly in the middle of your chest and the lower end tilts toward the left side of the body.

WHAT IS THE HEART MADE OF?

The heart is made of a special kind of muscle, called cardiac (heart) muscle, which never gets tired.

HOW OFTEN DOES BLOOD GO AROUND THE BODY?

Blood goes around the body about once a minute or 1,500 times a day.

WHAT IS PLASMA?

Just over half the blood is a yellowish liquid called plasma. It is mainly water with molecules of digested food and essential salts dissolved in it.

WHAT IS A CAPILLARY?

Blood travels around the body through tubes called arteries and veins. These branch off into smaller and smaller tubes that reach every cell of the body. Capillaries are the tiniest blood vessels of all. Most capillaries are thinner than a single hair. If an adult's capillaries were laid end to end they would stretch 60,000 miles—nearly 2.5 times around the world.

BLOOD IN CLOSE-UP

RED BLOOD CELL

PLASMA

WHAT JOB DOES YOUR HEART DO?

The heart's job is to pump blood to the lungs and then all around the body. The right side of the heart takes in blood from the body and pumps it to the lungs. The left side of the heart takes blood filled with oxygen from the lungs and pumps it to the rest of the body. Valves inside the heart stop blood flowing the wrong way. You can feel your heart beat if you put your hand on your chest.

"Used" blood leaves the heart for the right lung along the right pulmonary artery.

HOW OFTEN DOES THE HEART BEAT?

A child's heart usually beats about 80 times a minute, a bit faster than an adult's (70 times a minute). When you run or do something strenuous, your heart beats faster to send more blood to the muscles.

Blood stocked with oxygen enters the heart from the right lung along the right pulmonary veins.

WHAT ARE BLOOD GROUPS?

There are four main groups of blood, called groups A, B, AB, and O. Only some groups can be mixed with others, so doctors find out which blood group a patient belongs to before giving a blood transfusion.

The right side of the heart takes in "used" blood and pumps it to the lungs.

WHAT DO WHITE BLOOD CELLS DO?

White blood cells surround and destroy germs and other intruders that get into the blood.

WHY IS YOUR BLOOD RED?

Each tiny drop of your blood contains up to 5 million red blood cells that give blood its color. Red blood cells contain a substance called haemoglobin, which takes in oxygen in the lungs. Blood that is rich in oxygen is bright red. As this bright red blood is pumped around the body, the oxygen is gradually taken up by the body's cells. By the time the blood returns to the heart, it is a slightly darker, more rusty red.

WHITE BLOOD CELL

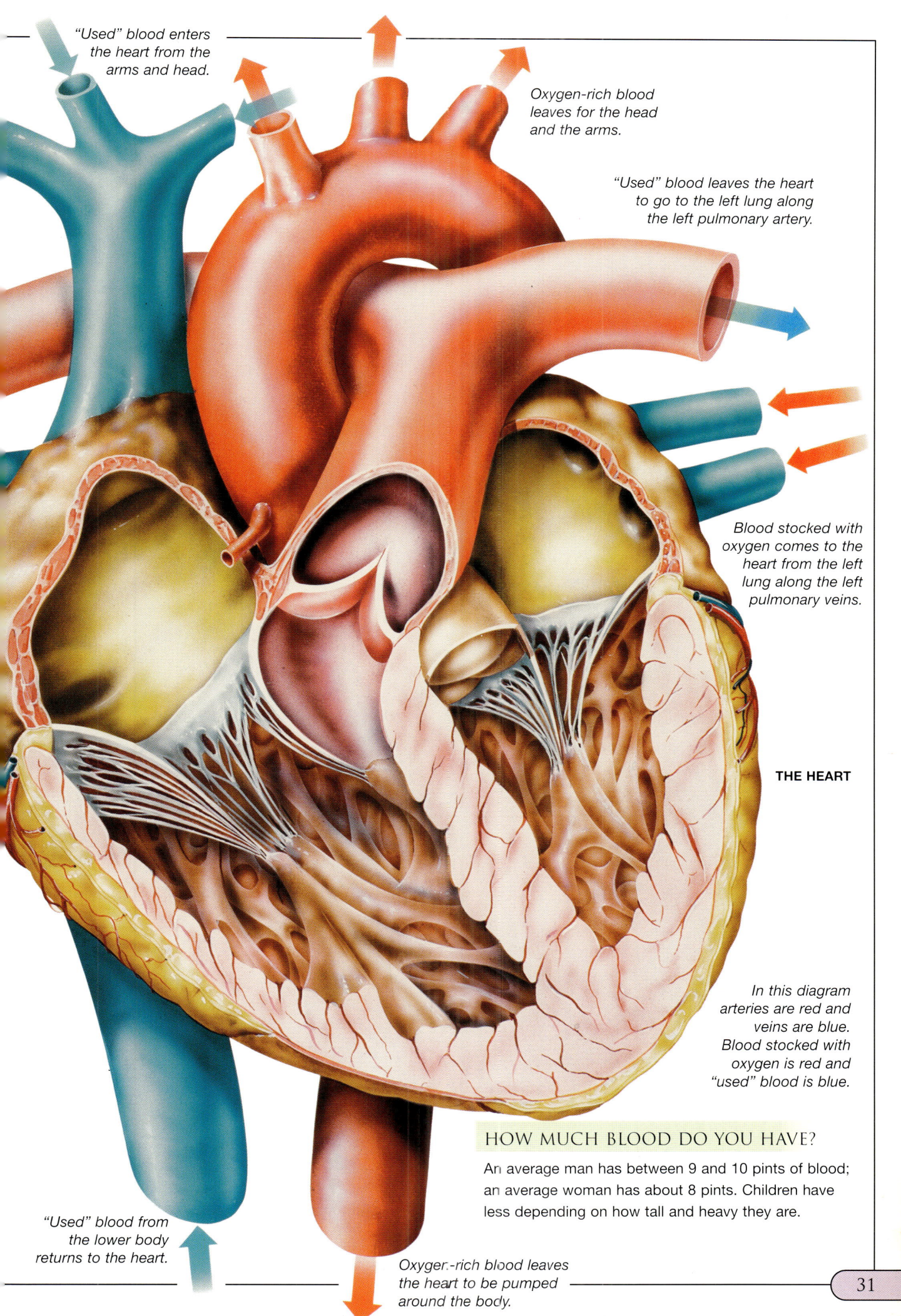

"Used" blood enters the heart from the arms and head.

Oxygen-rich blood leaves for the head and the arms.

"Used" blood leaves the heart to go to the left lung along the left pulmonary artery.

Blood stocked with oxygen comes to the heart from the left lung along the left pulmonary veins.

THE HEART

In this diagram arteries are red and veins are blue. Blood stocked with oxygen is red and "used" blood is blue.

HOW MUCH BLOOD DO YOU HAVE?

An average man has between 9 and 10 pints of blood; an average woman has about 8 pints. Children have less depending on how tall and heavy they are.

"Used" blood from the lower body returns to the heart.

Oxygen-rich blood leaves the heart to be pumped around the body.

WHAT DOES THE BRAIN DO?

Your brain controls your body. It keeps the heart, stomach, lungs, kidneys, and other vital organs working. The information collected by the senses is processed by different parts of the brain. Some is discarded, some is stored, and some is reacted to at once, with messages being sent from the brain to the muscles and glands. The brain also gives you your sense of who you are. Memories of the past are stored here and everything you think, feel, and do is controlled by the brain.

WHY ARE SOME PEOPLE LEFT-HANDED?

Most people are right-handed because the left side of their brain is dominant, but in left-handed people, the right side of the brain is dominant. The part of the brain that controls speech is usually on the dominant side.

WHAT IS THE BRAIN MADE OF?

The brain consists of water and billions of nerve cells and nerve fibers. It is surrounded by protective coverings called the meninges.

WHY DO YOU REMEMBER SOME THINGS AND FORGET OTHERS?

On the whole you remember things that are important to you in some way. Some things need to be remembered for only a very short while. For instance, you might look up a telephone number, keep it in your head while you dial it, and then forget it completely.

WHAT DOES THE BRAIN LOOK LIKE?

The brain looks soft and grayish pink. The top is wrinkled like a walnut and it is covered with many tiny tubes of blood. The spinal cord links the brain to the rest of the body.

INSIDE THE BRAIN

The cerebral cortex covers most of the brain.

The front of the cortex is mainly involved with thinking and planning.

The hypothalamus controls hunger, thirst, and body temperature.

The pituitary gland controls growth and many other body processes.

SKIPPING

When you skip, your brain coordinates balance with the movements of your arms and legs.

WHY ARE SOME PEOPLE MORE ARTISTIC THAN OTHERS?

One side of the brain deals more with music and artistic skills, and the other side deals more with logical skills. How artistic or mathematical you are depends on which side of your brain is dominant (stronger).

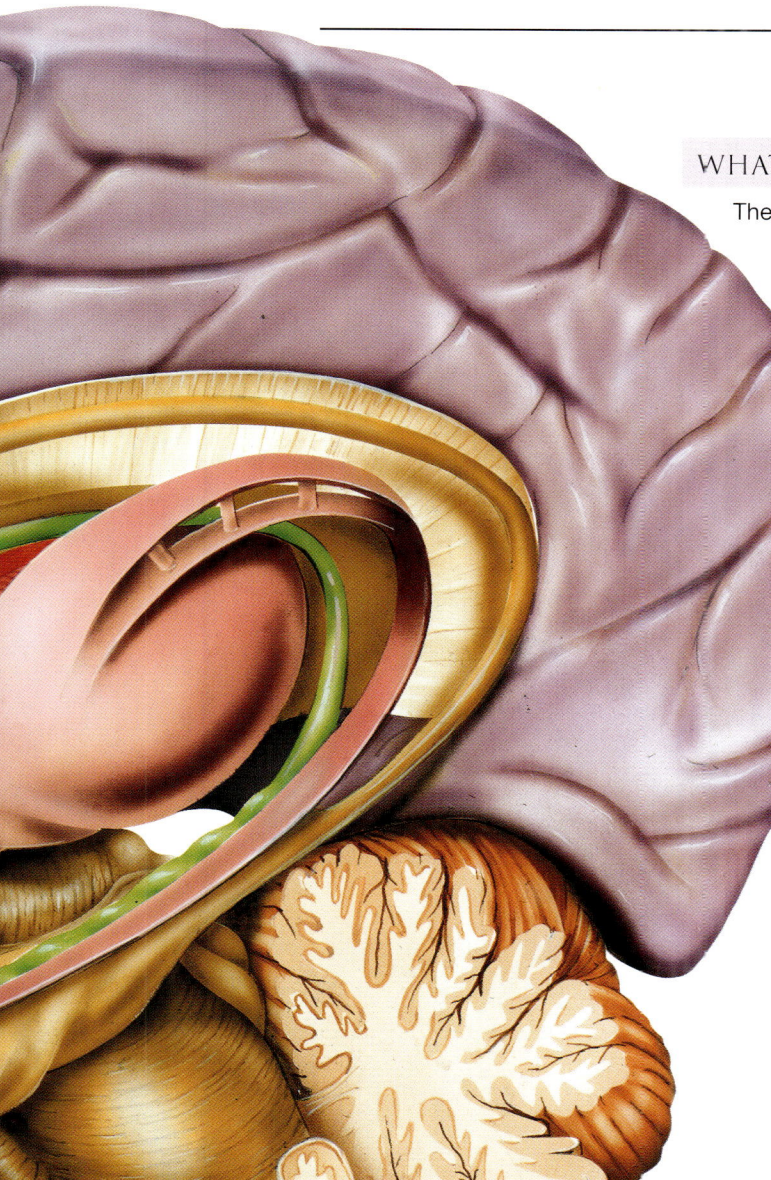

WHAT DOES THE CEREBRAL CORTEX DO?

The cortex is the wrinkly top part of the brain. It controls all the brain activity that you are aware of—seeing, thinking, reading, feeling, and moving. Only humans have such a large and well developed cerebral cortex. Different parts of the cortex deal with different activities. The left side controls the right side of the body, while the right side of the cortex controls the left side of the body.

WHY DO SOME PEOPLE SLEEPWALK?

People may walk in their sleep because they are worried or anxious. If someone is sleepwalking you should gently take them back to bed.

This part of the cortex deals with sight.

WHAT DOES THE SKULL DO?

The skull is a hard covering of bone that protects the brain like a helmet. All the bones of the skull except the lower jaw are fused together to make them stronger.

When you are asleep the brain blocks incoming signals unless they are so strong they wake you up.

The cerebellum coordinates movement and balance.

SLEEPING

DOES THE BRAIN EVER REST?

Even while you are asleep the brain carries on controlling body activities such as breathing, heartbeat, and digestion.

HOW OFTEN DO YOU DREAM?

You probably dream about five times every night, but you are only aware of dreaming if you wake up during a dream.

WHY DO YOU NEED TO SLEEP?

A 10-year-old sleeps on average nine or 10 hours a night, but sleep time can vary a lot between four and 12 hours. If you sleep for eight hours a night, that's a third of your life! You need to sleep to rest your muscles and to allow your body time to repair and replace damaged cells.

WHY DO PEOPLE HAVE DIFFERENT COLORED EYES?

The iris is the colored ring around the pupil. The color is formed by a substance called melanin—brown-eyed people have a lot of melanin, while blue-eyed people have very little.

HOW BIG IS YOUR EYEBALL?

An adult eyeball is about the size of a golf ball, but most of the eyeball is hidden inside your head.

WHY DOES THE PUPIL CHANGE SIZE?

The pupil becomes smaller in bright light to stop too much light from getting in and damaging the retina. In dim light the pupil opens to let in more light. The iris is a muscle that opens and closes the pupil automatically.

Light hits the retina at the back of the eye.

The cornea is a tough see-through layer that protects the eye.

The iris is a circular muscle that controls the size of the pupil to allow light into the eye.

The lens focuses light.

Muscles hold and move the eyeball.

HOW DO THE EYES SEE THINGS?

You see something when light bounces off it and enters your eyes. The black circle in the middle of the eye is a hole, called the pupil. Light passes through the pupil and is focused by the lens on to the retina at the back of the eye. Nerve endings in the retina send signals along the optic nerve to the brain. The picture formed on the retina is upside down, but the brain turns it around so that you perceive things to be the right way up.

WHAT MAKES YOU CRY?

If dust or something gets into your eye, the tear gland above the eye releases extra tears to wash it away. Being upset can also make you cry.

The image of the object projected on to the retina at the back of the eye is upside down.

HOW LIGHT ENTERS THE EYE

WHY DO YOU BLINK?

You blink to clean and protect your eyes. Each eye is covered with a thin film of salty water, so every time you blink, the eyelid washes the eyeball and wipes away dust and germs. The water drains away through a narrow tube into your nose. You also blink to protect your eye when something comes too close to it. Blinking is so important, you do it automatically.

The optic nerve takes signals from the retina to the brain.

The eyeball is filled with jelly, which keeps it in shape.

The tear gland makes a constant supply of salty water.

The pupil is the black hole at the center of the iris.

When too much water floods the eye, some spills over as tears and the rest drains into the nose.

The tear duct drains tears to the nose.

HOW DO YOU SEE COLOR?

Different nerve cells in the retina react to the colors red, blue, and green. Together they make up all the other colors.

WHY CAN'T YOU SEE COLOR WHEN IT STARTS TO GET DARK?

The cells that react to colored light—called cones—only work well in bright light. Most of the cells in the eye see in black, white, and gray, and these—called rods—are the ones that work at night.

WHAT KEEPS THE EYE IN PLACE?

The eyeball is held firmly in place by six muscles attached to the top, bottom, and each side of the eye. These muscles work together to move your eyes so that you can look around.

CAN SUNSHINE DAMAGE THE EYE?

Sunshine contains ultraviolet rays, which can damage your eyes as well as your skin. You should wear sunglasses in bright sunlight and never, never look directly at the Sun.

WHAT IS THE BLIND SPOT?

The blind spot is a spot on the retina where the optic nerve leaves the eye. There are no light-sensitive cells here, making the spot "blind."

WHY DO YOU HAVE TWO EYES?

Two eyes help you to judge how far away something is. Each eye gets a slightly different picture, which the brain combines into a single three-dimensional or 3D picture. A 3D picture is one that has depth as well as height and breadth.

HOW DO YOU SMELL?

A smell is made by tiny particles in the air. As you breathe in, some of these particles reach the smell receptors in your nose. Smell receptors react to chemicals dissolved in the mucus inside your nose and send a message to the brain.

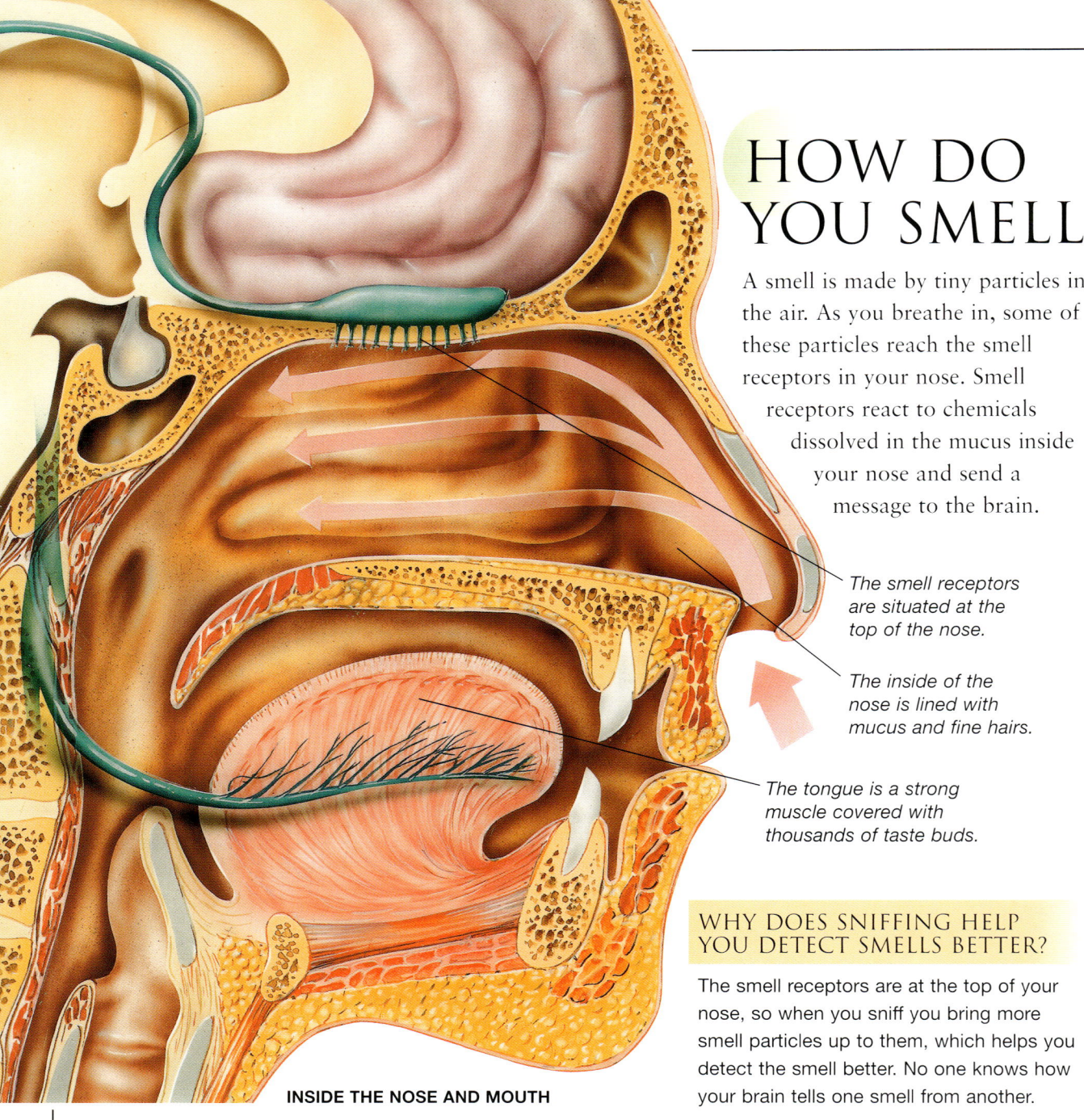

The smell receptors are situated at the top of the nose.

The inside of the nose is lined with mucus and fine hairs.

The tongue is a strong muscle covered with thousands of taste buds.

INSIDE THE NOSE AND MOUTH

WHY DOES SNIFFING HELP YOU DETECT SMELLS BETTER?

The smell receptors are at the top of your nose, so when you sniff you bring more smell particles up to them, which helps you detect the smell better. No one knows how your brain tells one smell from another.

WHY DO SOME THINGS SMELL MORE THAN OTHERS?

Things that smell strongly, such as perfume or food cooking, give off more smell particles that float through the air.

WHICH PARTS OF THE BODY ARE MOST SENSITIVE TO TOUCH?

Any part of the body that has lots of touch receptors is particularly sensitive to touch. These parts include the lips, tongue, fingertips, and soles of the feet.

HOW DOES THE SENSE OF TOUCH WORK?

The sense of touch tells you whether something is rough, shiny, wet, cold, and many other things. There are many different kinds of sense receptor in the skin, which between them react to touch, heat, cold, and pain. Some touch receptors react to the slightest thing, while others need a lot of pressure to make them respond. The brain puts together all the different messages to tell you how something feels.

WHY DO SOME ANIMALS HAVE KEENER SMELL?

Many animals rely on smell for finding food and smelling attackers. The inside of their nose is lined with many smell receptors, which are situated close to their nostrils.

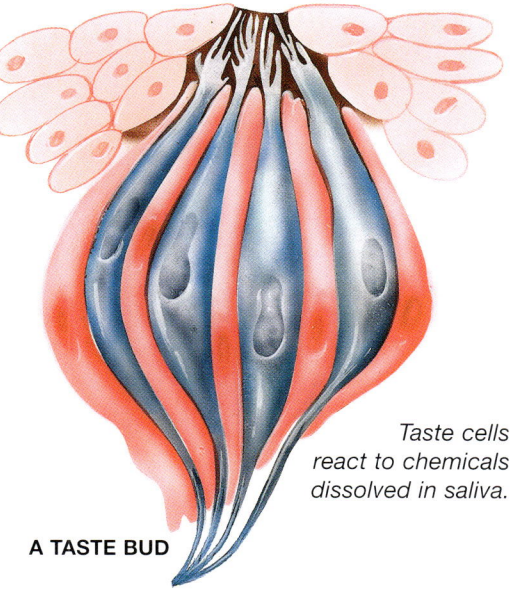

Taste cells react to chemicals dissolved in saliva.

A TASTE BUD

HOW DO YOU DETECT TASTE?

The surface of the tongue has about 10,000 microscopic taste buds sunk in it. As you chew, tiny particles of food dissolve in saliva and trickle down to the taste buds. The taste receptors react and send messages about the taste to the brain. There are four basic tastes—sweet, salty, bitter, and sour—and every taste is made up of one or a combination of these. The taste buds in different parts of the tongue react mainly to one of these basic tastes.

WHY DOES A BLOCKED NOSE STOP YOU TASTING?

When you eat, you both taste and smell the food. If your nose is blocked with mucus from a cold, you can't smell properly and so food seems to have less taste too.

DOES TASTE MATTER?

Unpleasant tastes can warn you when food has gone bad or is poisonous. Your body needs healthy food, so enjoying the taste of it encourages you to eat.

WHICH PARTS OF THE BODY ARE MOST SENSITIVE TO HEAT?

Your elbows and feet are more sensitive to heat than many other parts of the body. You may have noticed that bath water feels much hotter to your feet than it does to your hand. Your lips and mouth are very sensitive to heat too.

HOW DO BLIND PEOPLE USE TOUCH TO SEE?

Blind people can tell what something is like by feeling it. Outside, they may use a long cane to feel the way in front of them. Blind people read by touch: they run their fingertips over Braille—patterns of raised dots that represent different letters.

WHICH PART OF THE BODY IS LEAST SENSITIVE TO TOUCH?

The back is one of the least sensitive areas of the body.

WHY DO YOU LIKE SOME TASTES BETTER THAN OTHERS?

Most people prefer things that taste sweet or slightly salty, but your sense of taste can easily become used to too much sugar and salt. How you like food to taste is very much decided by your eating habits.

THE TONGUE

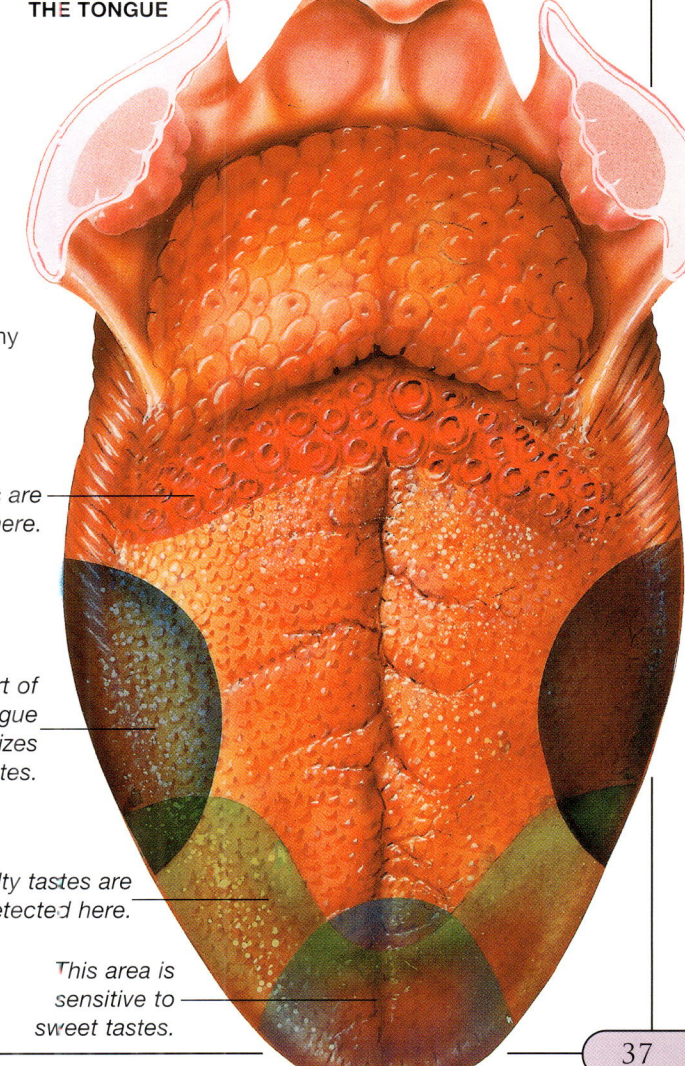

Bitter tastes are detected here.

This part of the tongue recognizes sour tastes.

Salty tastes are detected here.

This area is sensitive to sweet tastes.

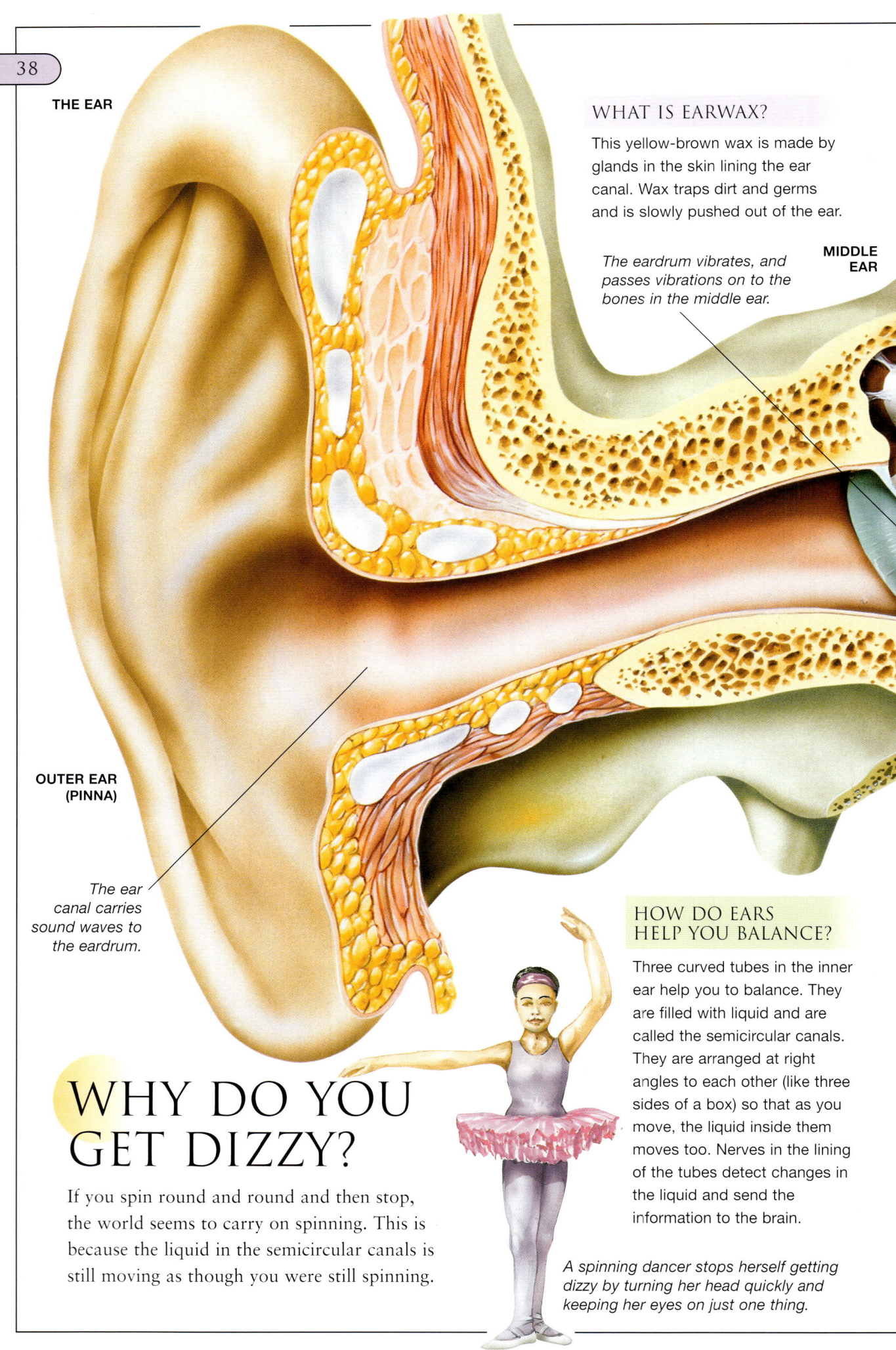

THE EAR

WHAT IS EARWAX?

This yellow-brown wax is made by glands in the skin lining the ear canal. Wax traps dirt and germs and is slowly pushed out of the ear.

The eardrum vibrates, and passes vibrations on to the bones in the middle ear.

MIDDLE EAR

OUTER EAR (PINNA)

The ear canal carries sound waves to the eardrum.

WHY DO YOU GET DIZZY?

If you spin round and round and then stop, the world seems to carry on spinning. This is because the liquid in the semicircular canals is still moving as though you were still spinning.

HOW DO EARS HELP YOU BALANCE?

Three curved tubes in the inner ear help you to balance. They are filled with liquid and are called the semicircular canals. They are arranged at right angles to each other (like three sides of a box) so that as you move, the liquid inside them moves too. Nerves in the lining of the tubes detect changes in the liquid and send the information to the brain.

A spinning dancer stops herself getting dizzy by turning her head quickly and keeping her eyes on just one thing.

The semicircular canals control balance.

The cochlea is filled with liquid and lined with nerve endings.

HOW DO YOU HEAR?

Sound reaches your ears as vibrations in the air. The vibrations travel down the ear canal to the eardrum, which then vibrates, making the bones in the middle ear vibrate too. These three small bones make the vibrations bigger and pass them through to the liquid in the inner ear. The cochlea in the inner ear is coiled like a snail shell. As nerve endings in the lining of the cochlea detect vibrations in the liquid inside it, they send electrical signals to the brain.

WHAT IS SOUND?

Sound is waves of energy that are carried as vibrations through air, liquid and solid objects.

IS LOUD NOISE DANGEROUS?

Any noise over about 120 decibels can damage your hearing immediately, but, if you are constantly listening to sounds of 90 decibels or more, they can damage your hearing too.

WHY DO YOU HAVE TWO EARS?

Two ears help you to detect which direction sounds are coming from.

HOW DO YOU MEASURE SOUND?

The loudness of a sound is measured in decibels. The sound of a pin dropping is less than 10 decibels, while the hum of a refrigerator is about 35 decibels. A loud personal stereo makes about 80 decibels while the noise of a jet aircraft just 90 feet away can reach 130 decibels.

INNER EAR

The Eustachian tube connects the middle ear to the top of the throat.

WHERE DOES THE EUSTACHIAN TUBE GO?

This tube joins the middle ear to the empty spaces behind your upper throat. If mucus from a cold fills the tube, it stops you hearing as well as usual.

HOW LOUD IS A WHISPER?

A whisper is between 10 and 20 decibels. Some animals can detect much quieter sounds than we can.

The noise of a jet aircraft just 90 feet away can reach 130 decibels.

A JET LIFTS OFF THE RUNWAY

THE MOMENT OF FERTILIZATION

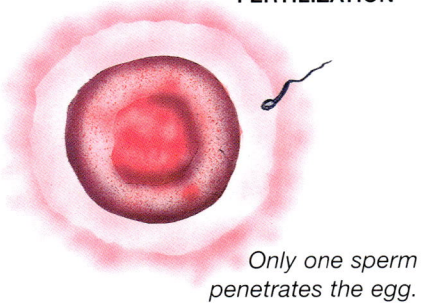

Only one sperm penetrates the egg.

WHERE DOES A MAN'S SPERM COME FROM?

Sperm are made in the testicles, two sacs that hang to either side of the penis. After puberty the testicles make millions of sperm every day. Any sperm that are not ejaculated are absorbed back into the blood.

WHERE DOES THE EGG COME FROM?

When a girl is born she already has thousands of eggs stored in her two ovaries. After puberty, one of these eggs is released every month and travels down the Fallopian tube to the womb.

WHAT ARE GENES?

Genes are a combination of chemicals contained in each cell. They determine everything about you, even what diseases you might get in later life.

WHY DO CHILDREN LOOK LIKE THEIR PARENTS?

You inherit a mixture of genes from your parents, so in some ways you will look similar to your mother, and in others to your father.

WHAT IS A PERIOD?

If the egg is not fertilized by a sperm, it passes out of the woman's body through the vagina. At the same time, the lining of the womb and some blood also pass out of the body. This slow flow of blood lasts about five days every month and is called a period.

WHAT IS A FETUS?

A fetus is an unborn baby from eight weeks after conception until birth. In the first seven weeks after conception it is called an embryo. By 14 weeks the fetus is fully formed, but it is too small and frail to survive outside the womb. Babies of 24 weeks can survive in an incubator if they are born early, but most stay in the womb for the full 36 weeks.

HOW DOES AN UNBORN BABY FEED?

Most of the cluster of cells that embeds itself in the womb grows into an organ called the placenta. Food and oxygen from the mother's blood pass through the placenta into the blood of the growing baby.

MALE REPRODUCTIVE ORGANS   **FEMALE REPRODUCTIVE ORGANS**

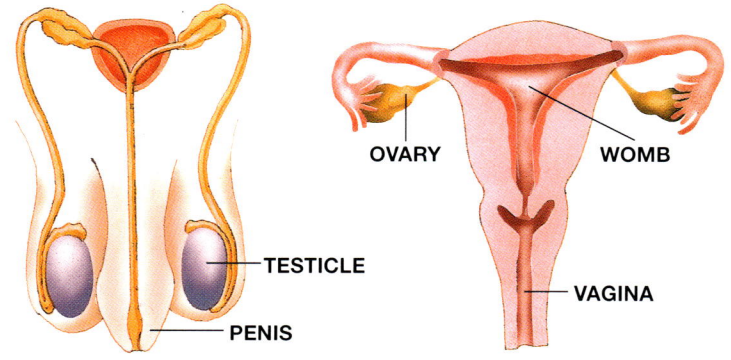

OVARY — WOMB

TESTICLE

VAGINA

PENIS

Testicles hang outside the body to keep the sperm cool.

The vagina joins the womb to the outside of the body.

WHAT DO BABIES DO IN THE WOMB?

As the unborn baby gets bigger, it exercises its muscles by kicking, moving, and punching. It also sucks its thumb sometimes, opens and shuts its eyes, and goes to sleep.

WHAT IS LABOR?

Labor is the process of giving birth. The neck of the womb stretches and opens, and then the womb, which is made of strong muscle, contracts to push the baby out. Labor takes several hours and can be very painful.

HOW DOES A NEW BABY BEGIN?

A new baby begins when a sperm from a man joins with an egg from a woman. This is called fertilization, and it happens after the man ejaculates sperm into the woman's vagina during sex. The cells of the fertilized egg begin to multiply into a cluster of cells, which embeds itself in the lining of the womb. There the cells continue to multiply and form the embryo of a new human being.

HOW FAST DOES AN UNBORN BABY GROW?

You grow faster before you are born than at any other time in your life. Three weeks after the egg is fertilized, the embryo is no bigger than a grain of rice. Five weeks later, almost every part of the new baby has formed—the head, brain, eyes, heart, stomach, and even the fingers—yet it is only about the size of a thumb. By the time it is born, 30 weeks later, it will probably be about 20 inches long and weigh about 7 lb.

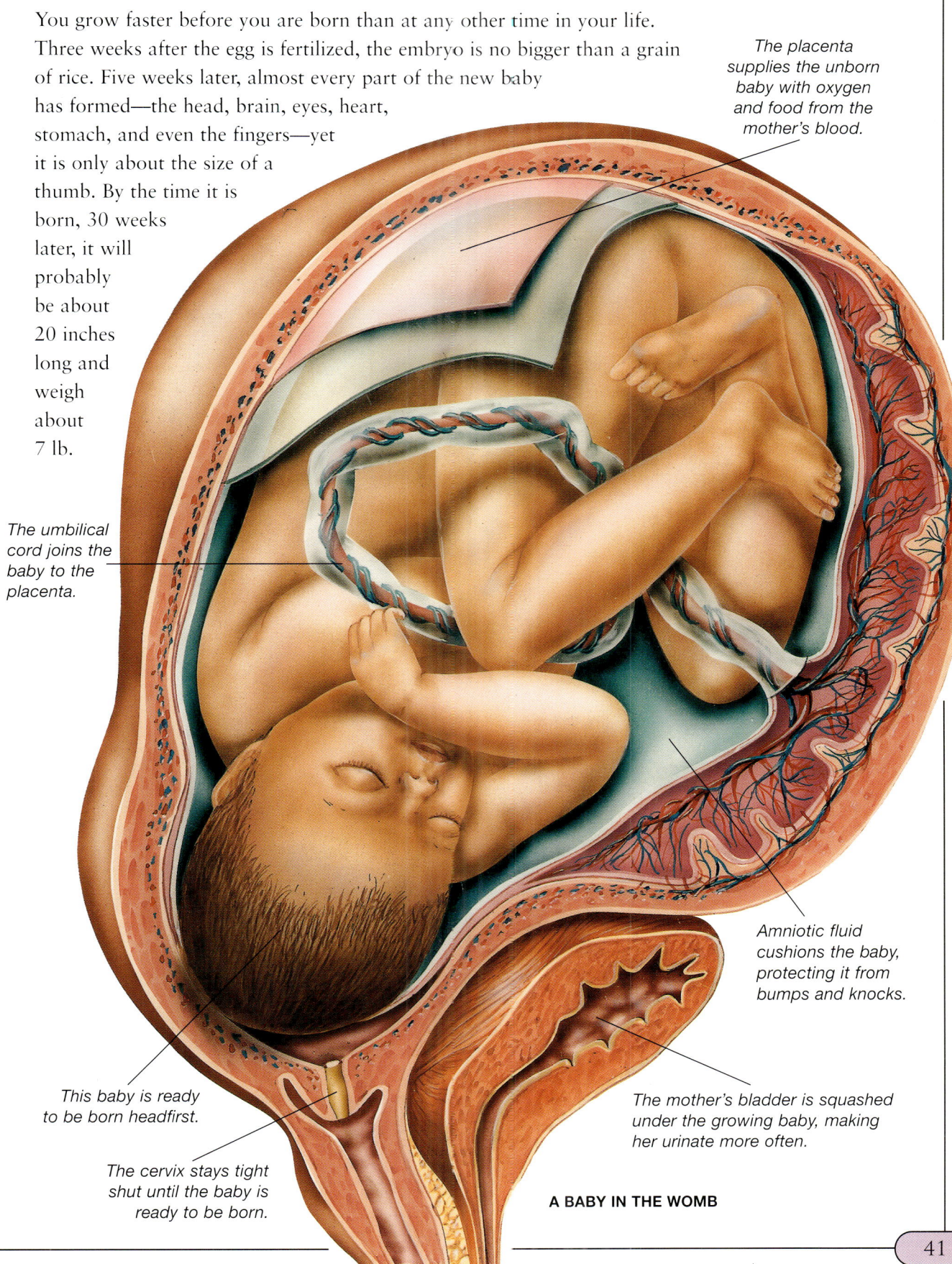

The placenta supplies the unborn baby with oxygen and food from the mother's blood.

The umbilical cord joins the baby to the placenta.

Amniotic fluid cushions the baby, protecting it from bumps and knocks.

This baby is ready to be born headfirst.

The mother's bladder is squashed under the growing baby, making her urinate more often.

The cervix stays tight shut until the baby is ready to be born.

A BABY IN THE WOMB

WHY DO PEOPLE AGE?

The cells of the body are constantly being renewed, except for brain cells and other nerve cells. As people get older, the new cells do not perform as well as the cells of younger people.

WHEN DO BABIES LEARN TO WALK AND TALK?

By its first birthday, a baby is usually already pulling itself up on to its feet and is nearly ready to walk. It may also be beginning to say a few words, though talking develops slowly over the next few years.

WHO HAD THE MOST CHILDREN?

It is believed that a Russian woman who lived in the 1700s holds this record. She was called Madame Vassilyev and she gave birth to no less than 69 children.

WHAT DO ALL NEW BABIES NEED?

All newborn babies need food, warmth, love, and protection. At first a baby can only drink liquids, so it sucks milk from its mother's breasts or from a bottle. Milk contains everything the new baby needs to grow and stay healthy. A baby also needs to be washed and have its diaper changed regularly. Babies sleep a lot of the time, but when they are awake they need plenty of smiles and cuddles. Babies and children rely on their parents for the things they need.

WHY DO YOU HAVE TO SUPPORT A YOUNG BABY'S HEAD?

When a baby is born the muscles in its back and neck are very weak, too weak to hold up its own head. A baby's head is much bigger for the size of its body than a child's or an adult's.

WHEN ARE YOU FULLY GROWN?

Boys and girls grow quickly during puberty, and then they grow more slowly until they reach their full height some time around age 20 years.

WHAT IS PUBERTY?

Puberty is the time in which you grow from a child into an adult. You grow taller and your body changes shape. A girl develops breasts and her hips become broader. Her waist looks thinner. A boy's chest becomes broader and his voice grows deeper. At the same time, the sex organs develop. A girl begins to have periods and a boy begins to produce sperm. Puberty lasts several years and affects moods, feelings, and attitudes as well as bringing physical changes.

During childhood, the legs and arms grow longer and the child becomes more adept and confident.

WHAT HAPPENS WHEN A BOY'S VOICE BREAKS?

A boy may be growing so fast during puberty that the muscles that control his vocal cords cannot keep up. His voice may suddenly change from high to low before finding the right pitch. The vocal cords also become thicker, making his voice deeper.

A two-year-old is about half the height it will be when adult.

Babies often learn to crawl before they take their first tottering steps.

WHAT IS THE MENOPAUSE?

The menopause is when a woman's body changes so that she is no longer able to have children. As sex hormone levels drop, her ovaries stop producing eggs. The woman may experience uncomfortable hot flushes and unpredictable mood swings.

WHAT MAKES YOU GROW?

A growth hormone tells your body to grow. This is produced in the pituitary gland in the brain and taken all round the body in the blood. Exactly how tall you grow is determined by genes inherited from your parents.

STAGES OF GROWTH

Adults are fully grown and may decide to have children of their own.

At puberty the sexual organs begin to mature.

WHAT ARE HORMONES?

Hormones are chemicals released into the blood from various glands. Some glands make sex hormones that control the menstrual cycle.

As people get older, they begin to slow down.

Very old people may become quite frail.

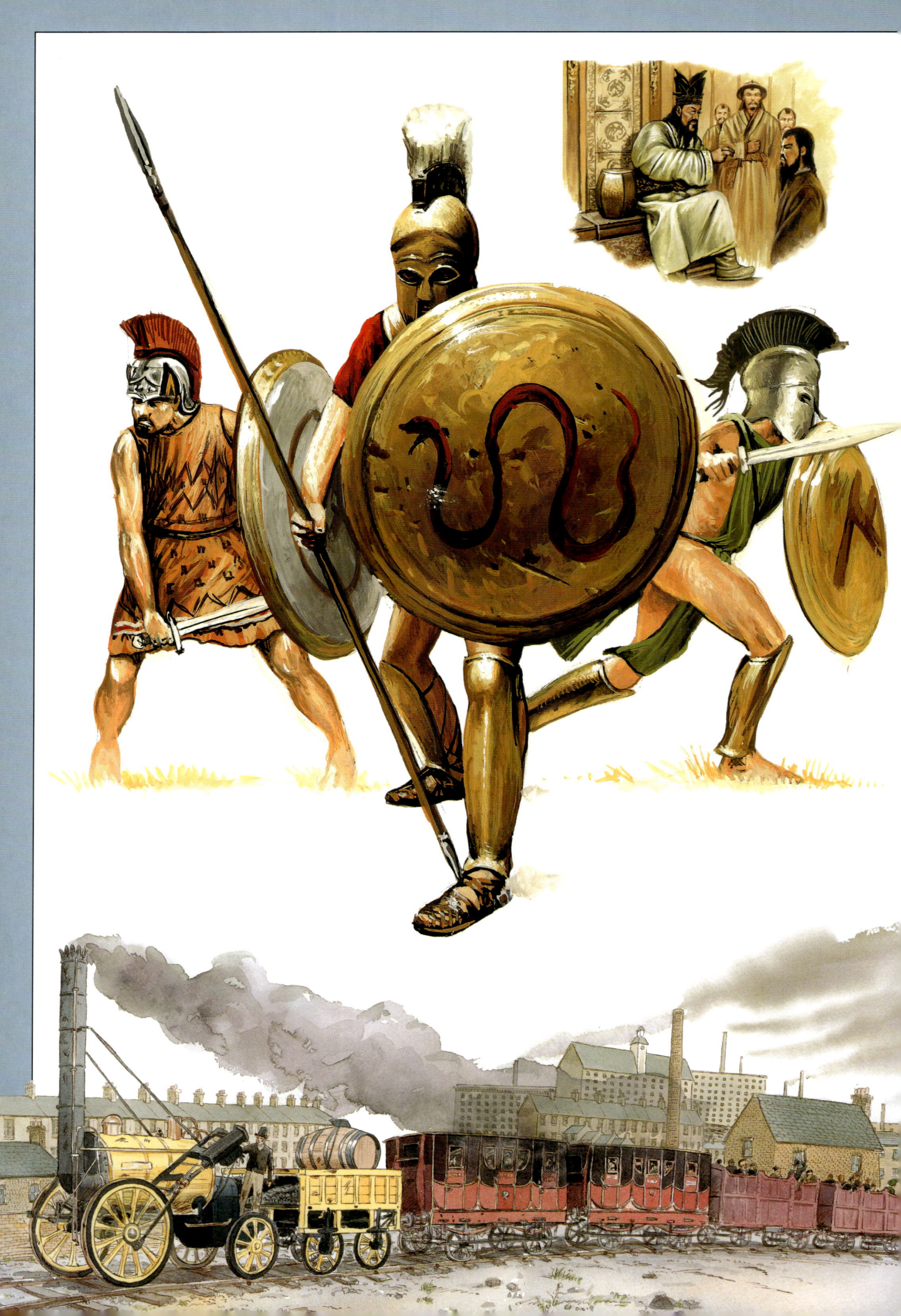

SECTION THREE

LOOKING
BACK

APE:
AUSTRALOPITHECUS

HOMINID:
HOMO HABILIS

HUMAN: HOMO
SAPIENS SAPIENS

This early human ancestor lived about 3 million years ago.

The first toolmaker lived about 2 million years ago.

Modern men and women first developed around 200,000 years ago.

HOW DID MODERN HUMANS DEVELOP?

Our distant ancestors are a group of animals known as primates. Primates first appeared on earth about 50 million years ago, and looked rather like squirrels. Over millions of years, they changed and grew as the environment changed around them and they learned new skills to adapt to it. Slowly, they developed into apes, then into hominids (almost-humans), then into modern human beings.

DID PEOPLE LIVE IN CAVES?

Yes, but not all the time. Nomad hunters built temporary shelters in cave entrances and used inner caves as stores. On hunting expeditions they camped in shelters made of branches, brushwood, dry grass, and bracken.

HOW DO WE KNOW ABOUT APES WHO LIVED MILLIONS OF YEARS AGO?

From fossil remains. Fossils are made when chemicals in the soil soak into dead bodies and turn the bones to stone. After many years, the soil turns into rock with fossils hidden inside.

WHO WERE THE NEANDERTHALS?

A type of human who lived in Europe and Asia from around 200,000 to 35,000 years ago. Neanderthals were short and stocky with low, ridged brows. They died out—no one knows why—and were replaced by modern humans, who originated in Africa.

WHAT DID PREHISTORIC PEOPLE WEAR?

In cold countries, they wore leggings and tunics made from furs and skins, sewn together using bone needles and sinews for thread. In hot countries, they wore skin loincloths—or nothing at all!

Hungry nomads set out from Siberia on the long trek to America.

WHEN DID PEOPLE START TO LIVE IN TOWNS?

Jericho in Jordan (built around 10,000 years ago) and Çatal Hüyük in Turkey (built around 8,000 years ago) are the world's first big towns. They were centers of trade and craftwork, and were surrounded by strong walls.

WHO WALKED TO AMERICA?

The first Americans! For millions of years, North and South America were cut off from the world by deep, stormy oceans. No one lived there. Then, during the last Ice Age, the oceans froze and parts of the sea-bed were uncovered. A "land-bridge" of dry seabed linked America and Northeast Asia. Many wild animals lived on the land-bridge, so groups of hunters roamed across it in search of food. Eventually, they reached America, and settled there. Historians are not sure exactly when this happened, but it was probably about 18,000 years ago.

THE FIRST AMERICANS

WHO LIVED IN HUTS MADE OF BONES?

Groups of nomads who lived on the plains of Eastern Europe about 15,000 years ago. They hunted woolly mammoths, ate the meat, and made shelters from the skin and bones.

ICE AGE HOME

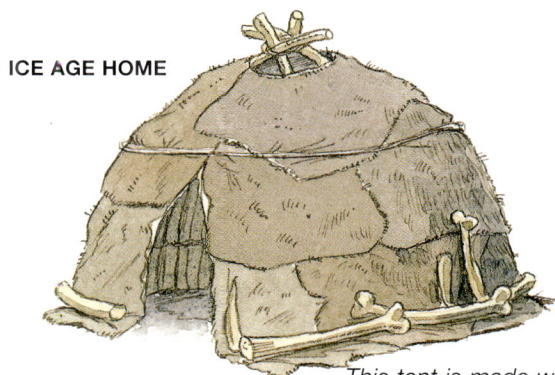

This tent is made with the skin and bones of the woolly mammoth.

WHERE WERE THE FIRST FARMS?

In the Middle East. About 11,000 years ago, people there noticed that wild grains they had accidentally scattered on the ground sprouted and grew into plants. So they cleared plots of land, scattered more grain, and harvested it when it was ripe.

WHEN DID PEOPLE START TO READ AND WRITE?

About 6,000 years ago. The Sumerians (who lived in present-day Iraq) were the first people to invent writing. They used little picture-symbols scratched on to tablets of soft clay. Only specially trained scribes could read them.

WHERE ARE THE PYRAMIDS?

In Egypt, in North Africa. They stand on the west bank of the River Nile. The Egyptians believed this was the land of the dead, because the Sun set there. They built their homes on the east bank of the river—the land of sunrise and living things.

Egyptian homes often had only one storey, with steps going up to the roof. They were usually made from mud-brick.

WHY WERE THE PYRAMIDS BUILT?

The pyramids are huge monumental tombs for pharaohs and nobility. The Egyptians believed that dead people's spirits could live on after death if their bodies were carefully preserved. It was specially important to preserve the bodies of dead pharaohs (Egyptian kings) and other nobles. Their spirits would help the kingdom of Egypt to survive. So they made dead bodies into mummies, and buried them in these splendid tombs along with clothes, jewels, and models of everything they would need in life after death.

WHAT WERE EGYPTIAN HOUSES LIKE?

Small and simple, with flat roofs that served as extra rooms and courtyards where people worked. Rich people's homes were large and richly decorated, with fine furniture, gardens, and pools.

HOW OLD ARE THE PYRAMIDS?

The first true pyramid was built around 2575 BC. Before then, people were buried under flat-topped mounds, called "mastabas," and in pyramids with stepped sides. The last pyramid was built around 1570 BC.

The pyramids" shape represented the rays of the Sun. The Egyptians believed that dead pharaohs were carried to heaven by the Sun's rays.

WERE ALL CORPSES MUMMIFIED?

EGYPTIAN COFFIN

No, because making a mummy was a complicated and expensive process. First, soft, internal organs like the stomach, lungs, and brain were removed, then the body was packed in natron (soda) for 40 days to dry out. Finally, it was wrapped in resin-soaked linen bandages, and placed in a beautifully decorated coffin. Most ordinary people were buried in simple coffins made of reeds, or sometimes just in shallow graves in the desert.

CARVED SCARAB

WHY DID EGYPTIAN PEOPLE CARRY CARVED STONE SCARABS?

Scarabs (dung-beetles) collected animal dung and rolled it into little balls. To the Egyptians, these dung balls looked like the life-giving Sun, so they hoped that scarabs would bring them long life.

WHICH HOUSEHOLD PETS GUARDED GRAIN STORES?

Cats! The Egyptians were probably the first people to tame cats. They encouraged wild cats to live on their farms, to kill the rats and mice that ate stores of grain. Later, Egyptians kept cats as pets in their homes. Can you guess the Egyptian word for cat? It was "miw!"

WHY WAS THE RIVER NILE IMPORTANT?

Because Egypt got hardly any rain. But every year the Nile flooded the fields along its banks, bringing fresh water and rich black silt, which helped crops grow. Farmers dug irrigation channels to carry water to distant fields.

The beautifully painted coffin protects the fragile mummy inside. Often, coffins were decorated with portraits of the dead person they contained.

WHAT WERE THE ORIGINAL OLYMPIC SPORTS?

At first, running was the only sport. Later, boxing, wrestling, chariot races, horse races, and pentathlon (running, wrestling, long-jump, discus, and javelin) were added. There were also music, poetry, and drama competitions.

Spartan soldiers were feared throughout Greece.

COULD WOMEN TAKE PART IN THE OLYMPIC GAMES?

No. Women were banned from the whole site during the games. But once every four years, there were special games for women only. They were held in honour of Hera, wife of the god Zeus.

DID THE GREEKS GO TO WAR?

Yes. In 490 BC and 479 BC, the Greeks defeated Persian invaders. From 431 BC to 362 BC, there were many civil wars. In 338 BC, Greece was conquered by the Macedonians, and Greek power ended.

WHICH CITY TRAINED THE BEST SOLDIERS?

Soldiers from the city of Sparta were said to be the bravest and best in all Greece. Spartan boys were taken away from their families when they were about eight years old, to learn how to fight and endure pain. They spent the next 25 years with the army!

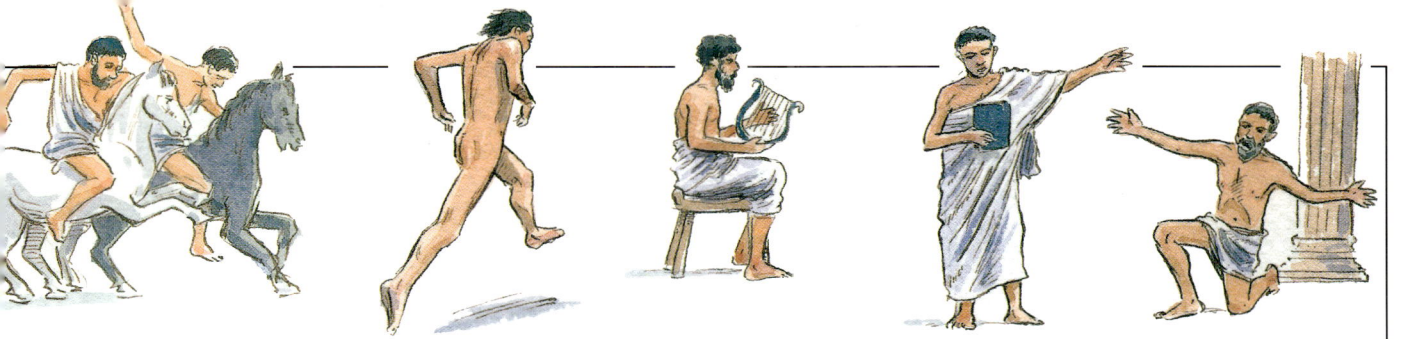

*The owl was the symbol
of the city of Athens.*

GREEK COINS

DID THE GREEKS INVENT MONEY?

No. The first coins were made in Lydia (part of present-day Turkey) around 600 BC. But the Greeks soon copied the Lydians and made coins of their own.

WHAT WERE GREEK COINS MADE OF?

Silver and gold. They were decorated with symbols of the cities where they were made, or with portraits of heroes and gods.

WHO WERE THE BARBARIANS?

Foreigners—people who did not speak Greek. The Greeks thought their words sounded like "baa, baa."

WHAT WERE GREEK WARSHIPS LIKE?

Long, narrow, and fast. They had a sharp battering ram at the prow, and were powered by 170 oarsmen and huge square linen sails. Sea battles were fought by ships smashing into one another, or by sailing close enough for men to jump across and fight on deck with swords and spears.

WHY DID THE GREEKS BUILD SO MANY TEMPLES?

Because they worshipped so many different goddesses and gods! The Greeks believed each god and goddess needed a home where their spirit could live. So they built splendid temples to house them, with beautiful statues inside. Each god and goddess had special powers, which visitors to the temple prayed for. Zeus was the god of the sky, Ares the god of war, and Aphrodite the goddess of love.

The Parthenon was dedicated to the goddess Athene.

THE PARTHENON, ATHENS

ROMAN CENTURION

Centurions were senior army officers. They dressed for parade in a beautifully decorated metal breastplate and a helmet topped with a crest of horsehair.

WHO WANTED TO RULE THE WORLD?

About 400 BC the Romans set out to conquer their Italian neighbors. By 272 BC they controlled all of Italy—but they didn't stop there! After defeating their rivals in Carthage (Northwest Africa), they invaded lands all around the Mediterranean Sea. In 31 BC they conquered the ancient kingdom of Egypt. They invaded Britain in 55–54 BC. By AD 117, in Emperor Trajan's reign, the mighty Roman Empire stretched from Scotland to Syria and to Iraq.

WHO JOINED THE ROMAN ARMY?

Young men from all over the empire. Recruits had to be fit, tall and strong, aged under 25, and (preferably) able to read and write. Roman citizens became legionary (regular) soldiers. Men from other nations enrolled as auxiliary (helper) troops.

DID THE ROMANS HAVE CENTRAL HEATING?

Yes. They invented a system called the "hypocaust." Hot air, heated by a wood-burning furnace, was circulated through brick-lined pipes underneath the floor.

HOW LONG DID ROMAN SOLDIERS SERVE?

For about 25 years. After that, they retired. They were given a lump sum of money, or a pension, and a certificate recording their service.

WERE THE ROMANS EXPERT ENGINEERS?

Yes—among the best in the world! They built roads, bridges, aqueducts (raised channels to carry water), long networks of drains and sewers, and the first-ever blocks of apartments.

WHO ATTACKED ROME WITH ELEPHANTS?

General Hannibal, leader of the Carthaginians, who lived in North Africa. In 218 BC he led a large army, including war-elephants, through Spain and across the Alps to attack Rome.

WHY DID THE ROMANS SPEND SO LONG IN THE BATH?

Because Roman baths were great places to relax and meet your friends. Most big towns had public bath-houses, with steam baths, hot and cold swimming pools, sports facilities, and well trained slaves giving massages and beauty treatments.

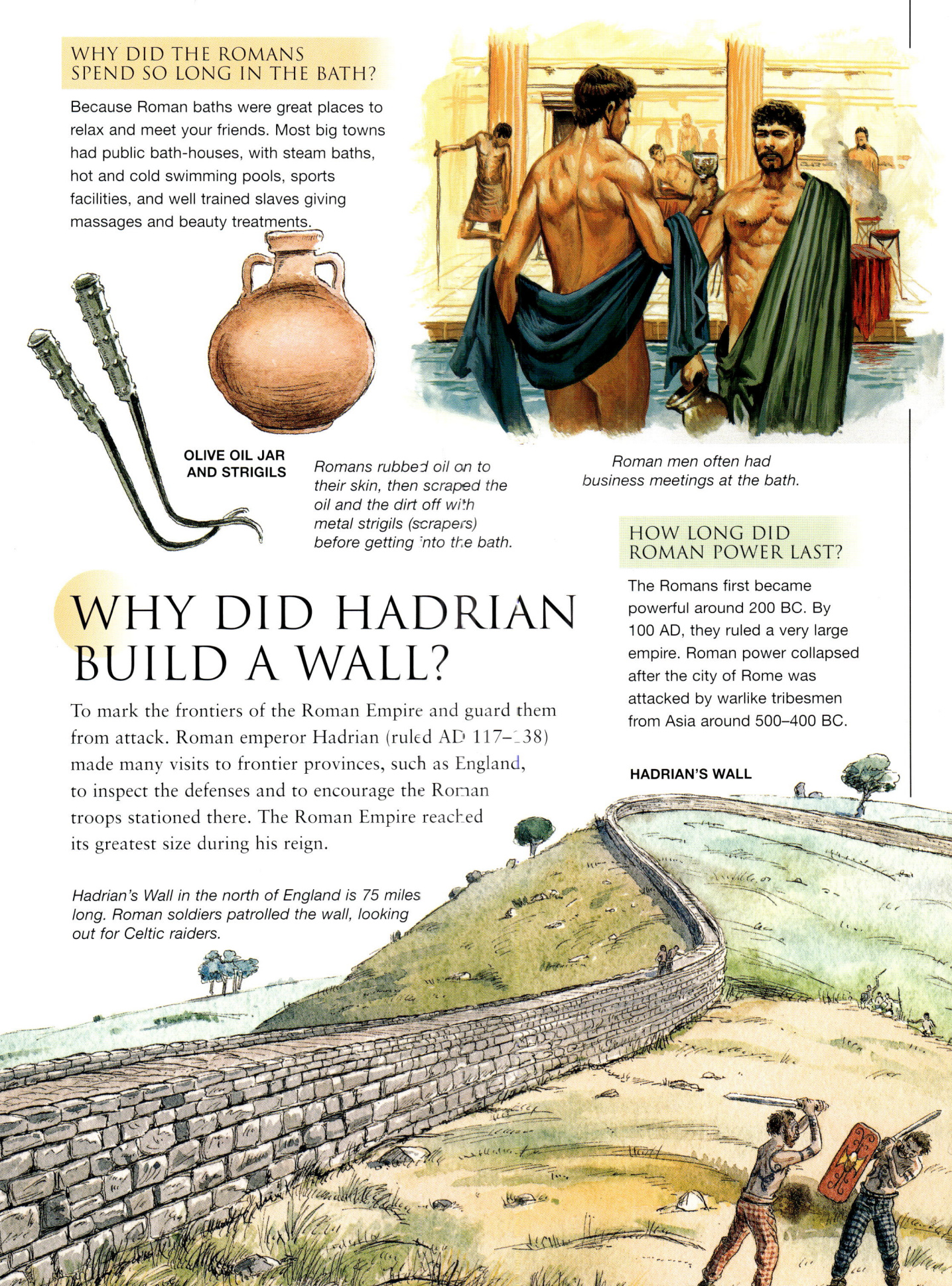

OLIVE OIL JAR AND STRIGILS

Romans rubbed oil on to their skin, then scraped the oil and the dirt off with metal strigils (scrapers) before getting into the bath.

Roman men often had business meetings at the bath.

HOW LONG DID ROMAN POWER LAST?

The Romans first became powerful around 200 BC. By 100 AD, they ruled a very large empire. Roman power collapsed after the city of Rome was attacked by warlike tribesmen from Asia around 500–400 BC.

WHY DID HADRIAN BUILD A WALL?

To mark the frontiers of the Roman Empire and guard them from attack. Roman emperor Hadrian (ruled AD 117–138) made many visits to frontier provinces, such as England, to inspect the defenses and to encourage the Roman troops stationed there. The Roman Empire reached its greatest size during his reign.

Hadrian's Wall in the north of England is 75 miles long. Roman soldiers patrolled the wall, looking out for Celtic raiders.

HADRIAN'S WALL

Incas gave gold offerings— like this model of a llama —to their gods.

INCA GOLD

WHAT WAS THE GOLDEN GARDEN?

A courtyard next to the Great Temple in the Incas' capital city of Cuzco. It contained lifesize models of animals and plants, made of real silver and gold. They were offerings to the gods.

WHO WAS THE "SON OF THE SUN?"

The Inca ruler—a king who was worshipped and feared. The Inca people believed he was descended from Inti, the Sun god. The greatest Inca leader was Pachachuti Yupanqui (ruled 1438–1471), who conquered many neighboring lands.

WHO CLIMBED UP STAIRWAYS TO GAZE AT THE STARS?

Priests and scribes belonging to the Maya civilization, which was powerful in Central America between around 200 and 900 AD. They built huge, step-sided pyramids, with temples and observatories on top. The Mayans were expert astronomers and mathematicians. They worked out very accurate calendars, and invented a system of numbers using just three symbols—shells, bars, and dots.

WHAT WAS A HUACA?

An Inca holy place. Inca people believed that powerful spirits lived in huacas in mountains, rivers, and caves. They left offerings there, to bring good luck. Rich nobles left food or clothes. Poor people left blades of grass, drops of water—or just an eyelash.

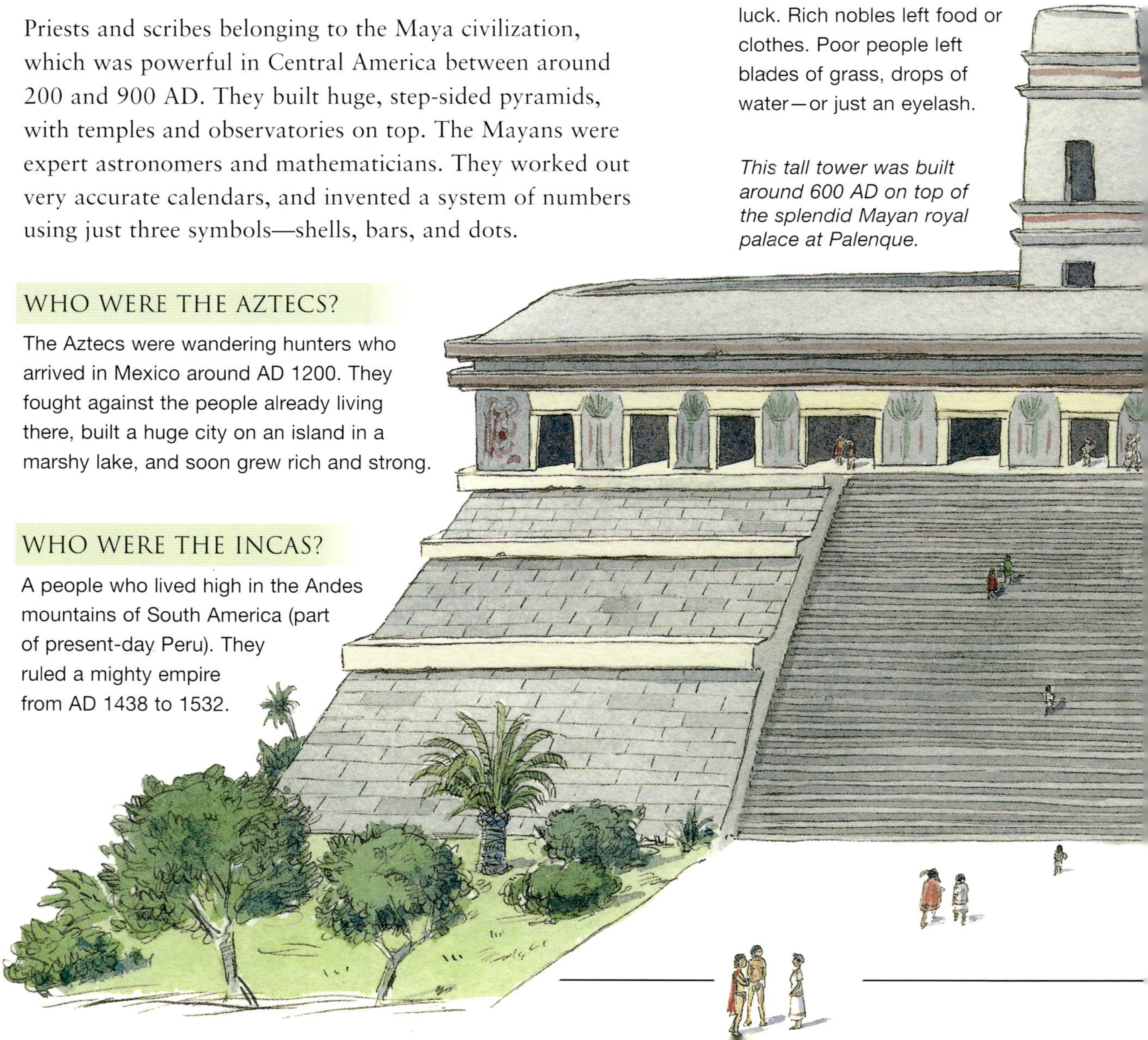

This tall tower was built around 600 AD on top of the splendid Mayan royal palace at Palenque.

WHO WERE THE AZTECS?

The Aztecs were wandering hunters who arrived in Mexico around AD 1200. They fought against the people already living there, built a huge city on an island in a marshy lake, and soon grew rich and strong.

WHO WERE THE INCAS?

A people who lived high in the Andes mountains of South America (part of present-day Peru). They ruled a mighty empire from AD 1438 to 1532.

WHO WAS THE GREAT FEATHERED SERPENT?

An important Aztec god—his real name was Quetzalcoatl. The Aztecs believed that one day, he would visit their homeland and bring the world to an end. Quetzalcoatl was portrayed in many Aztec drawings and sculptures. He was worshipped and feared by many other South American peoples, too.

Quetzalcoatl drawn by an Aztec scribe.

WHO FOUGHT THE FLOWERY WARS?

Fierce Aztec soldiers, armed with bows and arrows, knives and clubs. During the 15th and early 16th centuries, they fought against other tribes who lived in Mexico, in battles called the Flowery Wars. The Aztecs believed that the blood of their enemies fertilized the land and enabled flowers and crops to grow. They sacrificed prisoners of war and offered their hearts to the gods.

WHY WERE LLAMAS SO IMPORTANT?

Because they could survive in the Incas' mountain homeland, over 10,000 feet above sea level. It was cold and windy there, and few plants grew. The Incas wove clothes and blankets from llamas' soft, warm fleece, and used llamas to carry heavy loads up steep mountain paths.

WHO INVENTED CHOCOLATE?

Aztec cooks. They made a sweet, frothy chocolate drink from ground-up cocoa beans and honey, flavored with spices. We still use a version of the Aztec name for this drink— "chocolatl"—today.

WHAT WERE MAYAN PALACES MADE OF?

Great slabs of stone, or sun-dried mud brick, covered with a layer of plaster, then decorated with pictures of gods and kings. Mayan temples were built in the same way, but were painted bright red.

HOW DID THE MAYAS, AZTECS, AND INCAS LOSE THEIR POWER?

They were conquered by soldiers from Spain, who arrived in America in the early 16th century, looking for treasure—especially gold.

WHO WROTE IN PICTURES?

Mayan and Aztec scribes. The Mayans invented the first writing in America, using a system of picture symbols called glyphs. Mayans and Aztecs both wrote in zigzag folding books, called codexes, using paper made from fig-tree bark.

The massive stairway leads to the royal apartments, its doorways flanked by carvings of gods and kings.

MAYAN PALACE, PALENQUE

The Chinese emperor had supreme power over all of his people.

WHEN WAS THE FIRST CHINESE EMPIRE FOUNDED?

In 221 BC, all the separate Chinese states were united into one empire, ruled by the First Emperor, Shi Huangdi. He made many new laws; standardized Chinese writing, coinage, weights and measures; and gave orders for the Great Wall to be built to defend China.

A POTTERY MODEL OF A BULLOCK CART ON THE SILK ROAD

Carts were made of wood and woven bamboo, with strong wooden wheels.

WHERE DID THE SILK ROAD RUN?

From rich Chinese cities, across the Gobi desert, through the mountains of Central Asia to trading ports in the Middle East and around the Mediterranean Sea. European merchants traveled for years along the Silk Road to bring back valuable goods, especially silk and porcelain.

WHERE WAS THE MIDDLE KINGDOM?

The Chinese believed their country to be at the very center of the world, which is why they called it the Middle Kingdom. Certainly, for many centuries, China was one of the largest, richest, and most advanced civilizations anywhere on Earth. Under the Tang and Song dynasties (ruled AD 618–1279), for example, Chinese cities like Chang'an (present-day Xi'an) and Kinsai (present-day Huangzhou) were the biggest in the world, and very prosperous. At the same time, Chinese scientists and inventors made many important discoveries, including printing, porcelain, paper-making, rockets, gunpowder, banknotes, and clockwork.

WHO VALUED HONOR MORE THAN LIFE?

Japanese warriors, called samurai, who were powerful from around AD 1200. They were taught to fight according to a strict code of honor. They believed it was better to commit suicide rather than face defeat.

WHAT WAS CHINA'S BEST-KEPT SECRET?

How to make silk. For centuries, no one else knew how. Chinese women fed silk-moth grubs on mulberry leaves, and the grubs spun thread and wrapped themselves in it, to make cocoons. Workers steamed the cocoons to kill the grubs, unwound the thread, dyed it, and wove it into cloth.

Chinese potters left clay to weather for up to 40 years before firing (baking) at very high temperatures, until it was smooth as glass.

MING VASE

WHAT MADE CHINA SO PROSPEROUS?

The inventions of Chinese farmers and engineers made the land productive, and this made China wealthy. In the Middle Ages, the Chinese made spectacular strides in agriculture. They dug networks of irrigation channels to bring water to the rice fields. They built machines like the foot-powered pump (below) to lift water to the fields from canals. They also worked out ways of fertilizing fruit and vegetable plots with human manure.

WHICH RULERS CLAIMED DESCENT FROM THE SUN GODDESS?

The emperors of Japan. The first Japanese emperor lived around 660 BC; his descendants ruled until AD 1192. After that, army generals, called shoguns, ran the government, leaving the emperors with only religious and ceremonial powers.

HOW DID CHINA GET ITS NAME?

From fine pottery and porcelain, produced by Chinese workers, which was admired and valued in many parts of the world. Chinese potters pioneered many new techniques and designs. Some of their most famous pieces were decorated with blue-and-white glazes, like this tall jar, made around AD 1350.

Men worked for hours at this endless-chain machine. It forced water to flow uphill, pushed by wooden squares, to irrigate the fields.

FOOT-POWERED WATER PUMP

WHAT WAS THE INDUSTRIAL REVOLUTION?

It was a big change in the way people worked and goods were produced. It began around 1775 in Britain and spread to Belgium, Germany, northern Italy, France and—after 1850—to Japan, and the USA. Machines in huge factories replaced the craftworkers who used to make all kinds of goods slowly, one by one, at home. People had to learn new jobs operating machines that could mass-produce very large quantities of clothes, shoes, paper, metal, and wooden goods more quickly and cheaply than the hand-workers could.

WHO WORKED IN THE FIRST FACTORIES?

Thousands of poor, hungry, unemployed men and women moved from the countryside to live in fast-growing factory towns. They hoped to find regular work and more pay. Wages in factories were better than those on farms, and some people enjoyed the excitement and bustle of living in a town. But working conditions in factories were often dirty and dangerous, and houses in factory towns were crowded, noisy, and full of disease.

WHEN DID THE FIRST TRAINS RUN?

Horse-drawn railroad wagons had been used to haul coal trucks in mines since the 1600s, but the first passenger railroad was opened by George Stephenson in the north of England in 1825. Its locomotives were powered by steam. People rode standing in open carriages.

"THE ROCKET," BUILT BY GEORGE AND ROBERT STEPHENSON IN 1829

By 1900 many ordinary homes had lavatories, but only the rich could afford a polished wooden seat and an elaborately painted pottery pan like this.

LATE 19TH-CENTURY LAVATORY

WHY WERE DRAINS AND LAVATORIES SO IMPORTANT?

Because without them, deadly diseases carried in sewage could spread very quickly through crowded industrial towns. Pottery-making was one of the first mass-production industries. Machines in 19th-century pottery factories produced millions of cups, plates—and lavatory pans.

HOW DID RAILROADS CHANGE PEOPLE'S LIVES?

They helped trade and industry grow, by carrying raw materials to factories, and finished goods from factories to stores. They carried fresh foods from farms to cities. They made it easier for people to travel and encouraged a whole new tourism industry.

DID CHILDREN LEAD BETTER LIVES?

No. Many worked 16 hours a day in factories and down mines. Large numbers were killed in accidents with machinery, or died from breathing coal dust, cotton fibers, or chemical fumes. But after 1830, governments began to pass laws to protect child workers, and conditions slowly improved.

WHO MADE FIVE YEAR PLANS?

Joseph Stalin, Russian communist leader who ruled from 1924–1953. He reorganized the country in a series of Five Year Plans. He built thousands of new factories, took land away from ordinary people, and divided it into vast collective farms. Many of Stalin's schemes did not succeed; he used brutal punishments to silence his critics.

WHO DROPPED THE FIRST ATOMIC BOMB?

On August 6, 1945 the USA bombed Hiroshima, Japan, killing or wounding 150,000 people. By using this terrible new weapon on Japan, the USA, together with its allies in Britain and Russia, hoped to bring the Second World War (1939–1945) to an end. Japan was the strongest ally of Adolf Hitler, ruler of Nazi Germany. Hitler's invasions of European nations and his persecution of the Jewish people had led to the war breaking out in 1939. On August 14, Japan surrendered after the Americans dropped another atom bomb on the city of Nagasaki. The war was at an end.

MAO ZHEDONG

In 1966 Mao started a Cultural Revolution among the younger generation in China. He wrote down his thoughts in the "Red Book."

WHAT WAS THE LONG MARCH?

A grueling march by Chinese communist soldiers through wild, rocky countryside in 1934. They escaped from land held by their enemies and set up a communist state of their own. They were led by Mao Zhedong, who became ruler of all China in 1949.

A time of dangerous tension from 1947 to 1989 between the USA and the USSR—the two strongest nations on Earth. They had very different political systems and they distrusted and feared one another. The USA believed in freedom and big business; the USSR was communist. The superpowers never fought face to face, but they encouraged wars between smaller nations as a way of increasing their power.

MUSHROOM CLOUD

HOW HAS THE WORLD CHANGED SINCE 1900?

In many ways! European empires in Asia have collapsed, and new independent nations have taken their place. Women now play an important part in government. New scientific knowledge has saved millions of lives; cars and planes make travel faster than ever before; and phones, televisions, and computers send information rapidly all round the world. There are new dangers too—over-population, mass terrorism, and pollution. But in some ways, the world has hardly changed at all. Sadly, there is still a vast gap in living standards between rich and poor. And there are still many wars being fought.

MAN ON THE MOON

American astronaut, Neil Armstrong, was the first person to walk on the Moon, on July 20, 1969.

Atomic explosions create huge mushroom-shaped clouds of boiling gas and give off deadly, invisible radiation.

WHO COMPETED IN THE SPACE RACE?

The USSR and the USA. Each tried to rival the other's achievements in space, because they hoped to prove that their nation was best. The USSR took the lead by launching the first satellite in 1957 and the first manned space flight in 1961, but America won the race by landing the first man on the Moon in 1969.

SECTION FOUR

COUNTRIES AND THEIR PEOPLES

HOW DIFFERENT ARE WE FROM ONE ANOTHER?

All human beings are basically the same, wherever they live. We may speak different languages and have different ideas. We may wear different clothes and eat different foods. Our parents may give us dark or pale skin, blue eyes or brown, or various colors of hair. But in the end we share the same needs, pleasures, hopes, and fears.

6 billion people live on Earth.

HAVE HUMANS CHANGED OUR PLANET?

Over the ages, humans have changed the face of the world we live in. They have chopped down forests and dammed rivers. They have grown new plants and killed wild animals. They have built big cities and roads.

HOW MANY PEOPLE LIVE IN THE WORLD?

Billions! In 1997 there were about 5,840,000,000 human beings living on our planet. That's more than twice as many as 50 years ago.

WHAT IS A CONTINENT?

The big masses of land that make up the Earth's surface are called continents. The biggest continent of all is Asia, which is home to over 3.5 billion people.

WHERE DO PEOPLE LIVE?

Humans live wherever they can find food and water, which they need to stay alive. Nobody at all lives in Antarctica, the icy wilderness at the bottom of the world. Scientists do visit bases there, so that they can study rocks and icebergs and penguins. The Sahara desert in Africa is a land of burning hot sand and rocks. It has just a few places, called oases, where people can get the water they need to survive.

Some parts of the world are too harsh, too hot, or cold for people to settle.

FROZEN ARCTIC WASTES

WHO ARE THE WORLD'S PEOPLES?

Human beings who share the same history or language make up "a people" or "ethnic group." Sometimes many different peoples live in just one country. Over a hundred peoples live in Tanzania, each with its own way of life.

ARE THERE MORE AND MORE PEOPLE?

Every minute, 167 babies are born around the world. Imagine how they would cry if they were all put together! By the year 2025 there will probably be 8,036,000,000 people in the world.

WHY ARE SOME LANDS RICHER THAN OTHERS?

Some lands have good soil, where crops can grow. Some have oil, which is worth a lot of money. But other countries have poor soil, little rain, and no minerals. However hard people work there, they struggle to survive.

HAVE PEOPLE ALWAYS LIVED WHERE THEY DO NOW?

During history many peoples have moved huge distances, or migrated. The Polynesian people took 2,500 years or more to sail across the Pacific Ocean and settle its islands. People are still on the move today.

WHICH COUNTRY HAS THE MOST PEOPLE?

More people live in China than anywhere else in the world. They number about 1,237,000,000 and most of them live in the big cities of the east and the south. In the far west of China there are empty deserts and lonely mountains.

Places where many people have chosen to settle have become big cities.

WHERE ARE THE MOST CROWDED PLACES IN THE WORLD?

Tiny countries and large cities may house many millions of people. The most crowded of the bigger countries is Bangladesh, with over 800 people for every square kilometer of land.

NEW YORK CITY, USA

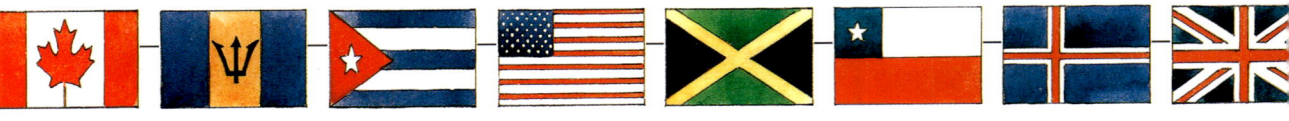

WHAT IS A COUNTRY?

A country is an area of land under the rule of a single government. A country may be vast, or very small. Its borders have to be agreed with neighboring countries, although this does sometimes lead to arguments. Countries that rule themselves are called independent. Countries that are ruled by other countries are called dependencies. Sometimes several countries join up to form a single new nation, but countries may also break up into smaller nations, too.

KURDISH REFUGEES

WHY DO COUNTRIES HAVE FLAGS?

Flags can be seen flying from buildings and from boats. They show bold patterns and bright colors as they flutter in the wind. Many flags are badges or symbols of a nation, or of its regions. The designs on flags sometimes tell us about a country or its history. The flag of Kenya includes a traditional shield and spears, while the flag of Lebanon includes the cedar tree, which brought wealth to the region in ancient times.

WHERE CAN YOU SEE ALL THE FLAGS OF THE WORLD?

Rows and rows of flags fly outside the headquarters of the United Nations in New York City, USA. Most of the world's countries belong to this organization, which tries to solve all kinds of problems around the world.

Refugees are people who have fled their country because of war or hunger.

HOW MANY INDEPENDENT COUNTRIES ARE THERE?

There are 192 independent countries in the world today. The number may change from one year to the next.

HOW MANY DEPENDENCIES ARE THERE IN THE WORLD?

Sixty-five of the world's nations are still ruled by other countries. They include many tiny islands in the Caribbean Sea and in the Atlantic and Pacific Oceans.

DO ALL PEOPLES HAVE A LAND THEY CAN CALL THEIR OWN?

No, the ancient homelands of some peoples are divided up between other countries. The lands of the Kurdish people are split between Turkey, Iran, and Iraq.

WHICH IS THE BIGGEST COUNTRY IN THE WORLD?

The gigantic Russian Federation takes up over 6 million square miles of the Earth's surface. It covers two continents, Europe and Asia, and its clocks are set at 11 different times.

Russia is so huge that when the Sun is setting over Moscow, it is rising over Vladivostock, on the Pacific coast.

HOW LONG DOES IT TAKE TO CROSS RUSSIA?

It depends how you travel! These days, trains on the famous Trans-Siberian railroad take eight days from Moscow to the Pacific coast.

CROSSING THE WORLD'S BIGGEST COUNTRY, 50 YEARS AGO

The Trans-Siberian railroad was built over a hundred years ago and opened in 1905.

WHICH COUNTRY FITS INSIDE A TOWN?

The world's smallest nation is an area within the city of Rome, in Italy. It is called Vatican City and is headquarters of the Roman Catholic Church. Only a thousand or so people live there.

SWISS GUARD, VATICAN CITY

WHAT ARE COUNTIES AND STATES?

If you look at the map of a country, you will see that it is divided up into smaller regions. These often have their own local laws and are known as states, provinces, counties, or departments.

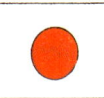

A DOGON VILLAGE, MALI

Mud huts and grain stores are built around a yard, or compound.

WHERE DO THEY BUILD MUD HUTS?

Thatched huts with walls of dried mud can still be seen in parts of Africa, such as Mali. They are cheap to build, cool to live in, and they often look beautiful too.

WHY WERE SKYSCRAPERS INVENTED?

So that more people could fit into a small area of city. High-rise apartments and offices were first built in Chicago, USA, about 120 years ago. By 1887 new high-speed elevators were saving people a very long climb upstairs!

WHICH PEOPLE LIVE IN CARAVANS?

Many of Europe's Gypsies live in caravans, moving from one campsite to another. The Gypsies, who are properly known as Roma, Sinti, or Manush, arrived in Europe from India about 1,000 years ago.

WHERE DO PEOPLE LIVE IN CAVES?

The first human beings often took shelter in caves. Even today, some people in Turkey and in China still make their homes in caves. These are not cold and dripping, like Stone Age dwellings. They can be snug and very comfortable.

WHAT ARE HOUSES MADE FROM?

Mud, stone, slate, boulders, bricks, branches, reeds, steel girders, sheets of iron, concrete, glass, timber planks, straw, scrap metal, turf, frozen snow, bamboo, animal hides, packing cases, cardboard boxes—you name it! All over the world people make use of whatever materials they can find or produce in order to build shelters and homes. Today many modern buildings look much the same wherever they have been built, from Brasília to Singapore. However, all sorts of local types of houses can still be seen as well.

WHY DO PEOPLE LIVE IN TENTS?

In many parts of the world people do not live in the same place all year round. They are nomads, following their herds of sheep and goats from one desert oasis to another, or from lowland to mountain pastures. The Bedouin are nomads who live in the dry lands of North Africa and the Near East. Their tents are woven from camel hair. Today some Bedouin have settled in towns.

Bedouin nomads use camels to move from one part of the desert to another.

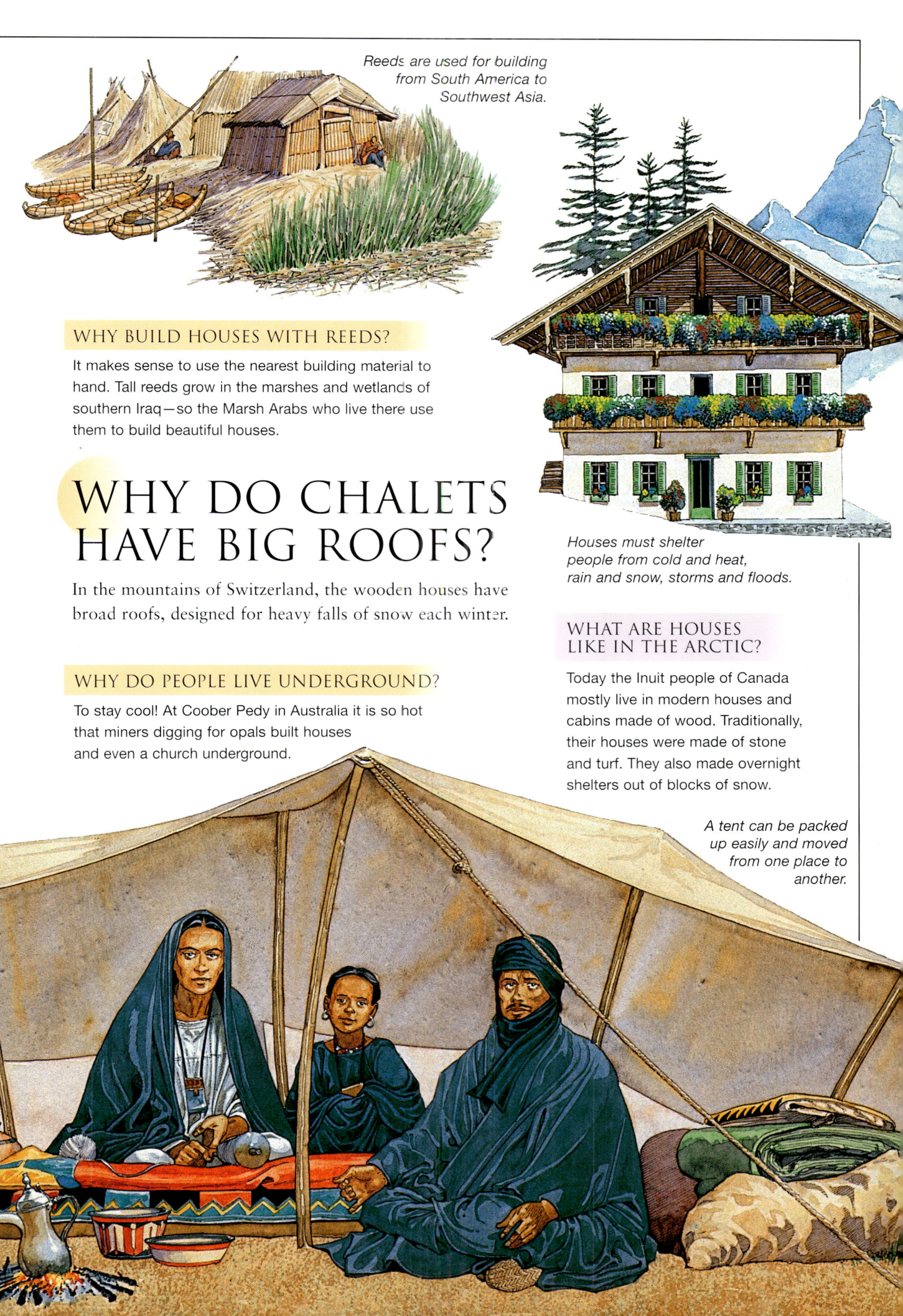

Reeds are used for building from South America to Southwest Asia.

WHY BUILD HOUSES WITH REEDS?

It makes sense to use the nearest building material to hand. Tall reeds grow in the marshes and wetlands of southern Iraq—so the Marsh Arabs who live there use them to build beautiful houses.

WHY DO CHALETS HAVE BIG ROOFS?

In the mountains of Switzerland, the wooden houses have broad roofs, designed for heavy falls of snow each winter.

WHY DO PEOPLE LIVE UNDERGROUND?

To stay cool! At Coober Pedy in Australia it is so hot that miners digging for opals built houses and even a church underground.

Houses must shelter people from cold and heat, rain and snow, storms and floods.

WHAT ARE HOUSES LIKE IN THE ARCTIC?

Today the Inuit people of Canada mostly live in modern houses and cabins made of wood. Traditionally, their houses were made of stone and turf. They also made overnight shelters out of blocks of snow.

A tent can be packed up easily and moved from one place to another.

SYDNEY, AUSTRALIA

The Sydney Opera House has become one of the best known buildings in the world. Many tourists come from all over the world to see it.

WHERE ARE THE BIGGEST CITIES IN THE WORLD?

In Japan, where big cities have spread and joined up to make giant cities! Japan is made up of islands that have high mountains, so most people live on the flat strips of land around the coast. In order to grow, large cities have had to stretch out like ribbons until they merge into each other. Over 27 million people live in and around the capital, Tokyo. It's still growing today. On the other side of the world, Mexico City is catching up fast.

WHICH IS THE HIGHEST CITY?

Lhasa stands 12,086 feet above sea level. It is the capital city of Tibet, a region in the Himalaya Mountains that is governed by China. Tibet is sometimes called the "roof of the world."

WHICH FAMOUS BUILDING LOOKS LIKE A SAILING BOAT?

Sydney Opera House is in Australia. Its roofs rise from the blue waters of the harbor like the sails of a big yacht.

Towns first grew up when people learned to farm. They no longer had to run after herds of wild animals for their food. They could stay in one place.

WHO LIVES AT THE ENDS OF THE EARTH?

One of the world's most northerly settlements is Ny-Alesund, in the Arctic territory of Svalbard. The southernmost is Puerto Williams in Tierra del Fuego, Chile.

WHY ARE LANDMARKS USEFUL IN A CITY?

Each city has eye-catching buildings and monuments, which help you find your way around. Paris, in France, has the Eiffel Tower. Berlin, in Germany, has the Brandenburg Gate.

ANCIENT ÇATAL HÜYÜK, TURKEY

WHAT PROBLEMS DO CITIES CAUSE?

Cities can be exciting places to live in. They are full of hustle and bustle. But they often have big problems, too. So many people in one place need a lot of looking after. They need water and electricity and proper drains, fire trucks and ambulances and police cars. Too much traffic often blocks up the roads and fills the air with fumes. In some countries people pour into the cities from the countryside. They cannot find work and have to live in poor conditions.

WHERE IS THE WORLD'S TALLEST BUILDING?

The Petronas Towers in Kuala Lumpur, Malaysia, look like two gigantic space rockets. They soar to nearly 1,483 feet, making up the tallest building in the world.

WHICH IS THE WORLD'S OLDEST CAPITAL?

Damascus, capital of Syria, has been lived in for about 4,500 years.

WHICH CITY IS NAMED AFTER A GODDESS?

Athens, the capital of Greece, shares its name with an ancient goddess called Athene. Her beautiful temple, the Parthenon, still towers over the modern city. It was built in 438 BC.

Cities became centers of trade, where people made pottery, baskets, food, tools, and clothes.

How does this ancient town differ from a modern one?

WHICH COUNTRY HAS THREE CAPITALS?

The most important city in a country is called the capital. South Africa has three of them! Cape Town is the home of the National Assembly. Pretoria is where the government offices are. Bloemfontein is the center for the law.

WHO BUILT THE FIRST CITIES?

The first cities were built in Southwest Asia. Çatal Hüyük in Turkey was begun about 9,000 years ago. It had buildings of mud brick, with flat roofs, and narrow streets. About 5,000 people lived there.

WHICH COUNTRY HAS THE MOST MOSLEMS?

Indonesia is the largest Islamic country in the world, although some parts of it, such as the island of Bali, are mostly Hindu.

Moslems pray to God (Allah) five times a day. The most important worship is at noon on Friday.

WHAT IS HANUKKAH?

This Jewish festival of light lasts eight days. Families light a new candle each day on a special candlestick called a menorah. Hanukkah celebrates the recapture of the temple in Jerusalem in ancient times.

MENORAH

WHY DO PEOPLE FAST?

In many religions people fast, or go without food, as part of their worship. If you visit a Moslem city such as Cairo or Algiers during Ramadan, the ninth month of the Islamic year, you will find that no food is served during daylight hours. Many Christians also give up eating certain foods during Lent, the days leading up to Holy Week, when they think about the death of Jesus. In Spain, during Holy Week, Christians carry crosses and religious statues in street processions.

WHICH CITY IS HOLY TO THREE FAITHS?

Jerusalem is a holy place for Jews, Moslems, and Christians. Sacred sites include the Western Wall, the Dome of the Rock, and the Church of the Holy Sepulchre.

WHICH PRIESTS COVER THEIR MOUTHS?

Some priests of the Jain religion, in India, wear masks over their mouths. This is because they respect all living things and do not wish to harm or swallow even the tiniest insect that might fly into their mouths.

WHY IS MOUNT ATHOS IMPORTANT?

This rocky headland in northern Greece is holy to Christians of the Eastern Orthodox faith. Monks have worshipped here since the Middle Ages. They wear beards, tall black hats, and robes.

WHO WAS CONFUCIUS?

This is the English name given to the Chinese thinker Kong Fuzi, who lived at the same time as Lao Zi. His beliefs in an ordered society and respect for ancestors became very popular in China.

WHAT IS SHINTO?

This is the ancient religion of Japan. At its holy shrines people pray for happiness and to honor their ancestors. Many Japanese people also follow Buddhist beliefs.

STAINED GLASS WINDOW

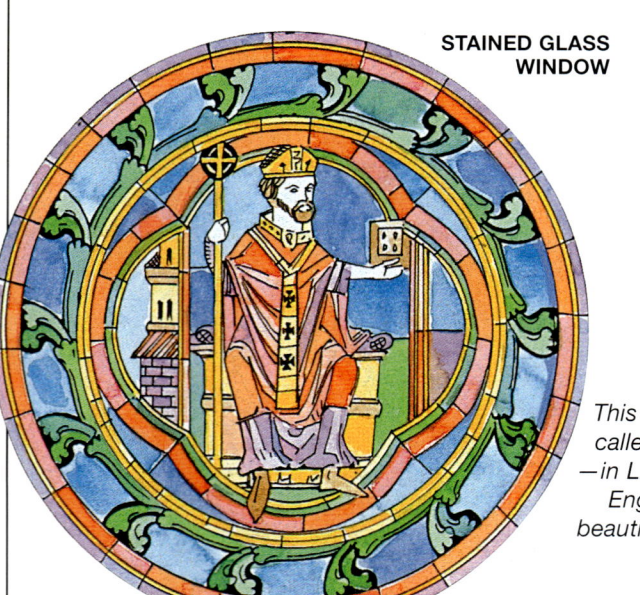

This round window — called a rose window — in Lincoln Cathedral, England, is made of beautiful stained glass.

WHERE DO PILGRIMS GO?

Pilgrims are religious people who travel to holy places and shrines around the world. Moslems try to travel to the sacred city of Mecca, in Saudi Arabia, at least once in their lifetime. Hindus may travel to the city of Varanasi, in India, to wash in the holy waters of the River Ganges. Christians travel to Bethlehem, the birthplace of Jesus Christ, or to the great cathedrals built in Europe during the Middle Ages, such as Santiago de Compostela in Spain.

Lighted candles mark the feast of Diwali. The Hindu religion grew up in India many thousands of years ago.

Light and fire are important symbols of the holy spirit in many religions.

WHAT IS THE TAO?

It is said "dow" and it means "the way." It is the name given to the beliefs of the Chinese thinker Lao Zi, who lived about 2,600 years ago. Taoists believe in the harmony of the universe.

WHERE DO YOUNG BOYS BECOME MONKS?

In Myanmar a four year-old boy learns about the life of Buddha at a special ceremony. He is cressed as a rich prince and is then made to wear the simple robes of a Buddhist monk.

WHAT ARE THE FIVE "K'S?"

Sikh men honor five religious traditions. Kesh is uncut hair, worn in a turban. They carry a Kangha, or comb, a Kkara or metal bangle, and a Kirpan or dagger. They wear an under-garment called a Kaccha.

WHAT IS DIWALI?

This is the time in the fall when Hindus celebrate their new year and honor Lakshmi, goddess of good fortune. Candles are lit in windows and people give each other cards and presents.

THE LAMPS OF DIWALI

**CROSSING THE
RUSSIAN ARCTIC**

HOW DO YOU CROSS THE ARCTIC SNOW?

You could always ride on a sled pulled by a team of dogs, as in the old days. But most people today ride snowmobiles, which are a bit like motorcycles with runners instead of wheels.

WHERE IS THE WORLD'S BIGGEST AIRPORT?

Riyadh airport in Saudi Arabia is bigger than some countries. It covers 87 square miles of the Arabian desert.

In Siberia, snowmobiles can use solid frozen rivers as roads during the winter months.

Traditional wooden boats still sail along the Hong Kong waterfront.

Many countries still use wooden boats. Dhows sail off Arabia and East Africa, and feluccas are used on the River Nile.

WHAT IS A JUNK?

It is a big wooden ship, traditionally built in China. Its big sails are strengthened by strips of wood. Junks aren't as common as they used to be, but they can still be seen on the South China Sea.

Hovercraft are used to carry passengers across fairly narrow stretches of water.

HOVERCRAFT

WHERE CAN YOU CATCH A TRAIN INTO THE SKY?

In the Andes mountains of South America. One track in Peru climbs to 15,807 feet above sea level. In Salta, Argentina, you can catch another high-rise locomotive, known as the "Train to the Clouds."

WHERE WAS A HOT-AIR BALLOON FIRST FLOWN?

The place was Paris, the capital of France, and the year was 1783. The passengers were, believe it or not, a sheep, a dog, and a duck! Later, people tried out the balloon for themselves.

HOW DOES A HOVERCRAFT WORK?

Large fans on a hovercraft suck in air and force it downward, where it is contained by a flexible skirt. Floating on this cushion of air, and driven by propellers, a hovercraft can travel over land or water. The fastest hovercraft can reach 65 mph.

A road train speeds across the Nullarbor Desert in southern Australia.

AUSTRALIAN ROAD TRAIN

WHERE ARE BOATS USED AS BUSES?

In the beautiful Italian city of Venice, there are canals instead of roads. People travel from one part of the city to another by boat.

CHINESE JUNK

WHERE ARE THE LONGEST TRUCKS?

In the outback, the dusty back country of Australia, the roads are long and straight and pretty empty. Trucks can hitch on three or four giant trailers to form a "road train."

WHAT IS THE WORLD'S LONGEST ROAD?

The Pan-American highway. It starts at the top of the world, in the chilly American state of Alaska. It then heads on through Canada and the USA to the steamy forests of Central America. There is still a bit missing in the middle, but the road starts up again and carries on all the way down through South America to Chile, looping round to Argentina and Brazil. The total distance? Well over 14,914 miles!

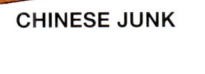

75

WHICH WERE THE FIRST ALL-AMERICAN CROPS?

Six hundred years ago, nobody in Europe had ever seen potatoes, maize, or tomatoes. These important food crops were first developed by the peoples who lived in the Americas before European settlers arrived there.

WHERE ARE THE WORLD'S BIGGEST RANCHES?

The world's biggest sheep and cattle stations are in the Australian outback. The best way to cross these lands is in a light aircraft.

Some rice terraces, like these in the Philippines, are thousands of years old.

WHAT IS A CASH CROP?

It is any crop that is sold for money. Many small farmers around the world can only grow enough food to feed themselves and their families, without having any to spare.

WHO ARE THE GAUCHOS?

The cowboys of the Pampas, which are the grasslands of Argentina. Once the Gauchos were famous for their wild way of life. Today they still round up the cattle on big ranches called estancias.

WHAT GROWS BEST IN FLOODS AND SOGGY WET MUD?

Rice keeps the world alive. Billions of people eat it every day, especially in Asia. Grains of rice are the seeds of a kind of grass that grows wild in wet river valleys. To cultivate it, farmers plant out the seedlings in flooded fields called paddies. In hilly lands, terraces are cut in the hillsides and the water flows down channels in the muddy soil.

TERRACED RICE FIELDS

COMBINE HARVESTER

Basic foods such as wheat (above) and rice are called staple crops.

WHERE ARE THE WORLD'S BREAD BASKETS?

Important wheat-producing areas of the world are called "bread baskets" because they provide us with the bread we eat each day. Wheat is a kind of grass, and so it grows best in areas which were once natural grasslands. These include the prairies of Canada and the United States and the steppes of Ukraine and southern Russia. Huge combine harvesters move across the prairies for days and weeks on end, cutting the wheat and separating out the grain.

SCOOP NETS

The fish swim into the nets when they are lowered into the water. The nets are then swung into the air and emptied.

ARE THERE ENOUGH FISH IN THE SEA?

Modern boats catch so many fish that in many places fish have become scarce. Some of the richest fishing grounds were off Newfoundland, in the North Atlantic Ocean. Fishing there has now been banned until the numbers recover.

Modern types of rice can produce several harvests a year. They can be planted by machines, but these are too expensive for many farmers.

WHERE DO FISHERMEN USE HOOPS AND SCOOPS?

Giant fishing nets like these can be lowered from the shore into lakes and seas. They are often used in China and India.

HOW CAN BARREN DESERTS BE TURNED GREEN?

Water can be piped into desert areas so that crops will grow there. But this irrigation can be very expensive and the water can also wash salts from the soil, making it difficult to grow plants.

WHERE DO FARMERS GROW COCONUTS?

Coconut fruits are big and green—the bit we buy in stores is just the brown seed inside. The white flesh inside the nut may be dried and sold as copra. Coconut palms grow best on the shores of the Indian and Pacific Oceans.

WHY DO PEOPLE LOVE TO DANCE?

MBUTI DANCERS

Dancing is a very dramatic way of expressing feelings of every kind. In Spain, passionate flamenco dancers stamp and click their fingers to guitar music. In England, morris dancers happily jingle bells tied to their legs and wave sticks. In Africa there are important dances for growing up and for funerals. The first dances of all were probably designed to bring good fortune to prehistoric hunters, where a priest put on the skins and horns of the animal his people wanted to kill.

WHO SINGS IN BEIJING?

Beijing opera is quite a performance! Musicians bang cymbals together and actors sing in high voices. They take the part of heroes and villains in ancient Chinese tales. Their faces are painted and they wear beautiful costumes with long pheasant feathers.

WHERE IS THE WORLD'S BIGGEST ART GALLERY?

At St Petersburg in Russia. It is made up of two great buildings, the Hermitage and the Winter Palace, and these hold millions of exhibits.

WHO MAKES PICTURES FROM SAND?

The Navaho people of the south-western United States make beautiful patterns using many different colored sands.

WHERE DO DRUMS TALK?

The tama is nicknamed the "talking drum." Its tightness can be varied while it is being played, to make a strange throbbing sound. It is played in Senegal and the Gambia, in Africa.

ABORIGINAL ART, AUSTRALIA

Like dance and theater, art often has its origins in religious and magical rituals.

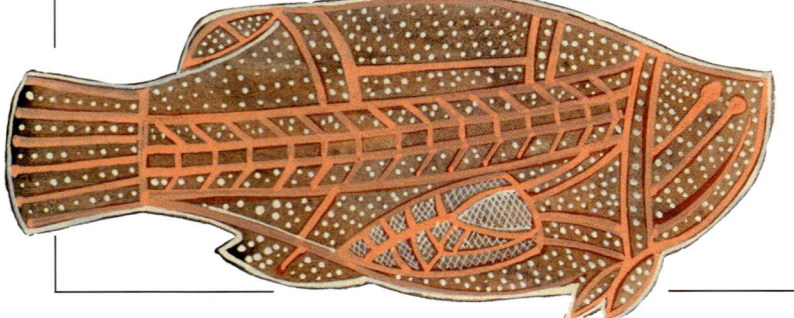

WHO PAINTS PICTURES OF THE DREAMTIME?

Australia's Aborigines look back to the dreamtime, a magical age when the world was being formed, along with its animals and peoples. They paint wonderful pictures of it.

WHERE DO THEY DANCE LIKE THE GODS?

Kathakali is a kind of dance drama performed in Kerala, southern India. Dancers in masks and gorgeous costumes act out ancient tales of gods and demons.

WHO DANCES A HAKKA?

In New Zealand young Maori people have kept alive many of their traditional dances. The hakka was a dance for warriors, to bring them strength to face the battles ahead.

WHO PLAYS THE "PANS?"

People in the Caribbean, at carnival time. The "pans" are the steel drums, which can produce beautiful dance rhythms and melodies.

WHAT IS KABUKI?

Kabuki is an exciting type of drama that became popular in Japan in the 1600s and may still be seen today. The actors wear splendid makeup and costumes.

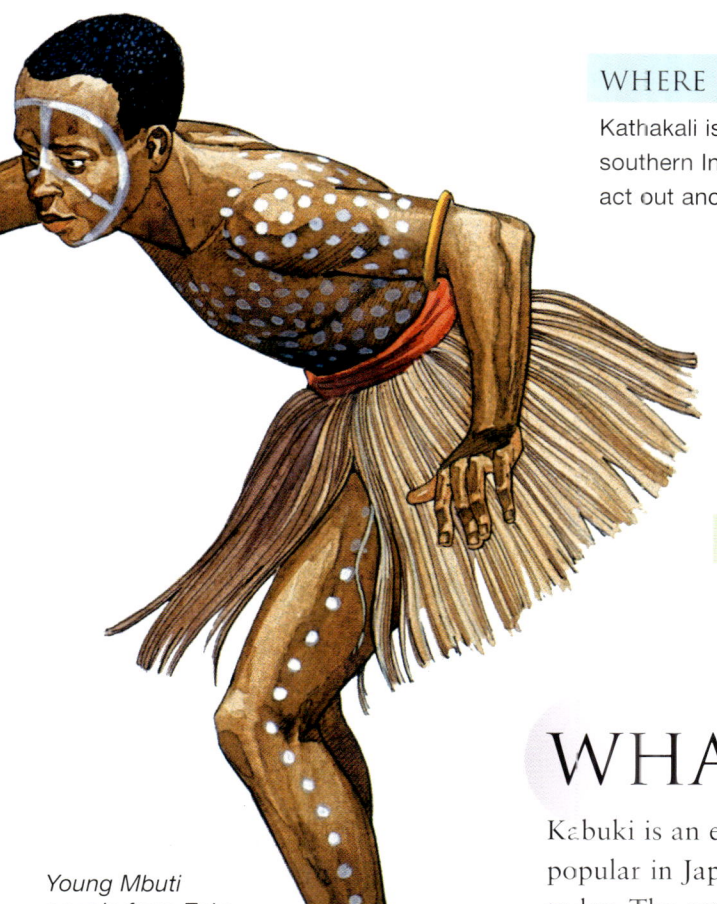

Young Mbuti people from Zaire decorate their bodies with white makeup for a dance to celebrate the beginning of adulthood.

KABUKI—JAPANESE THEATER

In kabuki, all the parts are played by male actors, some dressed up as beautiful women.

WHERE IS THE WORLD'S VERY OLDEST THEATER?

The oldest theater still in use today is called the Teatro Olimpico and it is at Vicenza, in Italy. It opened over 400 years ago. But people were going to see plays long, long before that. In ancient Greece people went to see masked actors appear in some of the funniest and saddest plays ever written, at open-air theaters made of stone. These can still be seen today all over Greece.

SECTION FIVE

MAGNIFICENT MACHINES

WHAT IS A MACHINE?

A machine is a piece of apparatus with several different parts—each with its own function—which uses the energy put into it to produce and direct force. People use machines to make different tasks possible or easier. Vehicles, tools, weapons, and musical instruments are all types of machine. A simple bicycle and a sophisticated satellite are both machines. In the building industry, machines range from basic pulleys to complex bulldozers, cranes, drills, and dump trucks.

HOW FAST IS A PAVER?

A paver is used to lay down a layer of hot tarmac on the surface of a road. This is a very slow process, and the paver moves at less than 0.65 mph as it performs its work.

TEREX TITAN

The world's largest truck—the Terex Titan.

WHY DOESN'T A CRANE FALL OVER?

Near the top of the crane's vertical tower, there are two horizontal arms, or "jibs." One is much longer than the other. The longer jib is used to lift heavy objects. The shorter, "counterweight" jib has large concrete blocks built into it. These balance the weight on the main jib and prevent the crane toppling over.

Tower cranes are designed to lift very heavy objects to great heights. They are mainly used in the construction of tall buildings.

HOW IS LIQUID CONCRETE DELIVERED TO THE TOP OF A BUILDING?

When a building is being constructed, the steel frame is built first. Liquid concrete is then poured into it to create floors and walls. A pump uses compressed air to force the concrete up a pipe so that it can be delivered at the required height.

TOWER CRANE

WHAT IS THE TEREX TITAN?

The Terex Titan 33-19 built by General Motors is the world's largest dump truck. It is nearly 56 feet long, and with a full load it weighs 605 tons. Its fuel tank can hold 1,566 gallons of diesel.

WHY DON'T SKYSCRAPERS FALL OVER?

Because skyscrapers are so tall, they need deep foundations to prevent them toppling over. At the foot of a skyscraper, builders drive steel girders called piles into the ground and set them in concrete. To hammer the piles in, they use a machine called a pile-driver, which is basically a very heavy weight on the end of a crane.

HOW IS AIR USED TO DRILL?

A pneumatic drill is powered by air. The air is put under pressure by a compressor, then fed to the drill through a rubber pipe. When the trigger of the drill is pressed, the compressed air is pushed into a cylinder just above the drill's blade or "bit." This forces the bit downward into the ground. Almost immediately, the air is released into another cylinder which pushes the bit back up. This all happens several times a second.

WHAT WAS THE FIRST PINBALL MACHINE?

All pinball machines originate from a Victorian game called bagatelle. The first pinball machine was introduced in 1930 and was called "Baffle Ball." It was an instant hit, and more than 50,000 were sold.

WHERE COULD PEOPLE LISTEN TO THE FIRST JUKEBOX?

The first jukebox was installed in the Palais Royal Saloon, San Francisco, USA, in 1889. But people were not allowed to make their own music selections! The first proper jukebox, where people could choose a song, arrived in 1915.

PINBALL MACHINE

Although pinball machines were first sold in 1930, they did not have flashing lights and illuminated scores until 1933. Bumpers were introduced in 1936.

WHAT WAS THE FIRST SUCCESSFUL COMPUTER GAME?

In 1971, Nolan Bushell designed Computer Space. Using the small profits from this game, Bushell constructed Pong for Atari, which was the first commercially successful arcade game.

HOW DOES A MACHINE MAKE MOVIES "MOVE?"

Images projected on a cinema screen are not really "moving" at all. Each film is made up of thousands of still pictures, or frames, each slightly different to the one before. When a projector turns the film fast enough, one frame merges into the next and the image appears to move. The audience's brains are fooled into seeing movement that is not actually there. This is because of something known as "persistence of vision."

WHEN WAS THE FIRST PERSONAL STEREO MADE?

Personal stereos were introduced in 1979 by the Sony Corporation. They called them "Walkman boogie-paks." Sony have since sold over 100 million of their little machines.

WHAT IS A TELEVISION PICTURE?

If you look closely at a television screen, you will see that it contains hundreds of horizontal lines. Each of these lines contains hundreds of different-colored dots. From a distance, these dots merge together to create the illusion of a complete picture. A television screen is only capable of showing three colors—red, green, and blue. These colors merge with each other to create all the different colors on the screen.

HOW CAN A LASER BEAM LISTEN TO MUSIC?

The surface of a compact disc or CD is made up of a spiral track containing billions of microscopic pits. A CD player shines a laser beam through the plastic on the bottom of the CD. The beam is reflected back by the CD's metal coating. The variations in this reflection, caused by the pits, are translated into sound by a microprocessor.

MINI HI-FI SYSTEM

A mini hi-fi system comprising a CD player, cassette deck, and radio connected to stereo loudspeakers.

WHAT IS AN ENDOSCOPE?

Doctors use an endoscope to look inside a patient's body. The endoscope is a long, thin tube containing two bundles of fiber-optic cables. It is inserted into the body, and light is bounced along one bundle. This light is reflected back along the other bundle, creating a detailed image of the tissue.

WHAT DOES MRI MEAN?

MRI stands for Magnetic Resonance Imaging. We are all filled with tiny biological magnets, and MRI uses these natural magnets to build up a picture of the inside of a patient's body. It is safer than an X-ray which produce radiation that is harmful in large amounts.

HOW DOES AN X-RAY MACHINE WORK?

X-rays are electromagnetic waves similar to light. X-rays can easily move through the skin of a patient but they are absorbed by bones and teeth. They are beamed through a patient's body on to photographic film, where the shadows of bones show up any fractures.

X-RAY MACHINE

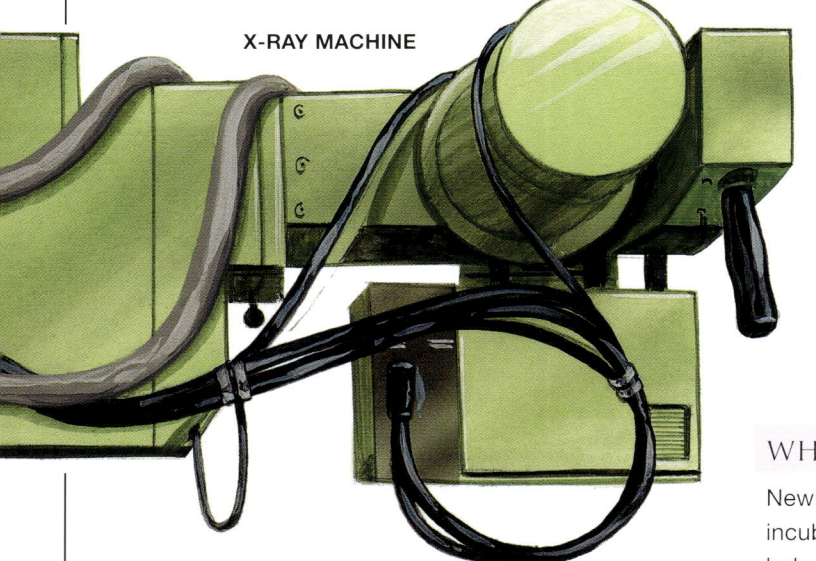

Hospitals use X-ray machines to check for broken bones. Dentists often use them too, to detect areas of decay in teeth.

HOW DOES A RESPIRATOR WORK?

Patients who have lost the use of muscles required for breathing can be placed inside a respirator. The air pressure inside the respirator is decreased causing the patient's chest to rise, which draws air into the lungs. The air pressure is then returned to normal and the chest falls, forcing out the air.

WHAT MACHINES LOOK AFTER BABIES?

Newborn babies can be placed in machines called incubators, which provide an ideal environment for a baby's health. The amount of oxygen, warmth, and humidity can all be regulated in an incubator, and germs can be kept out.

HOW CAN SOUNDS LOOK INSIDE A PATIENT'S BODY?

A machine called an ultrasound scanner sends sound waves into the patient's body, and uses a sensor to detect "echoes" of these sounds. These echoes are used to build up a picture on a screen. Ultrasounds are often used to look at an unborn baby.

X-RAY OF HAND

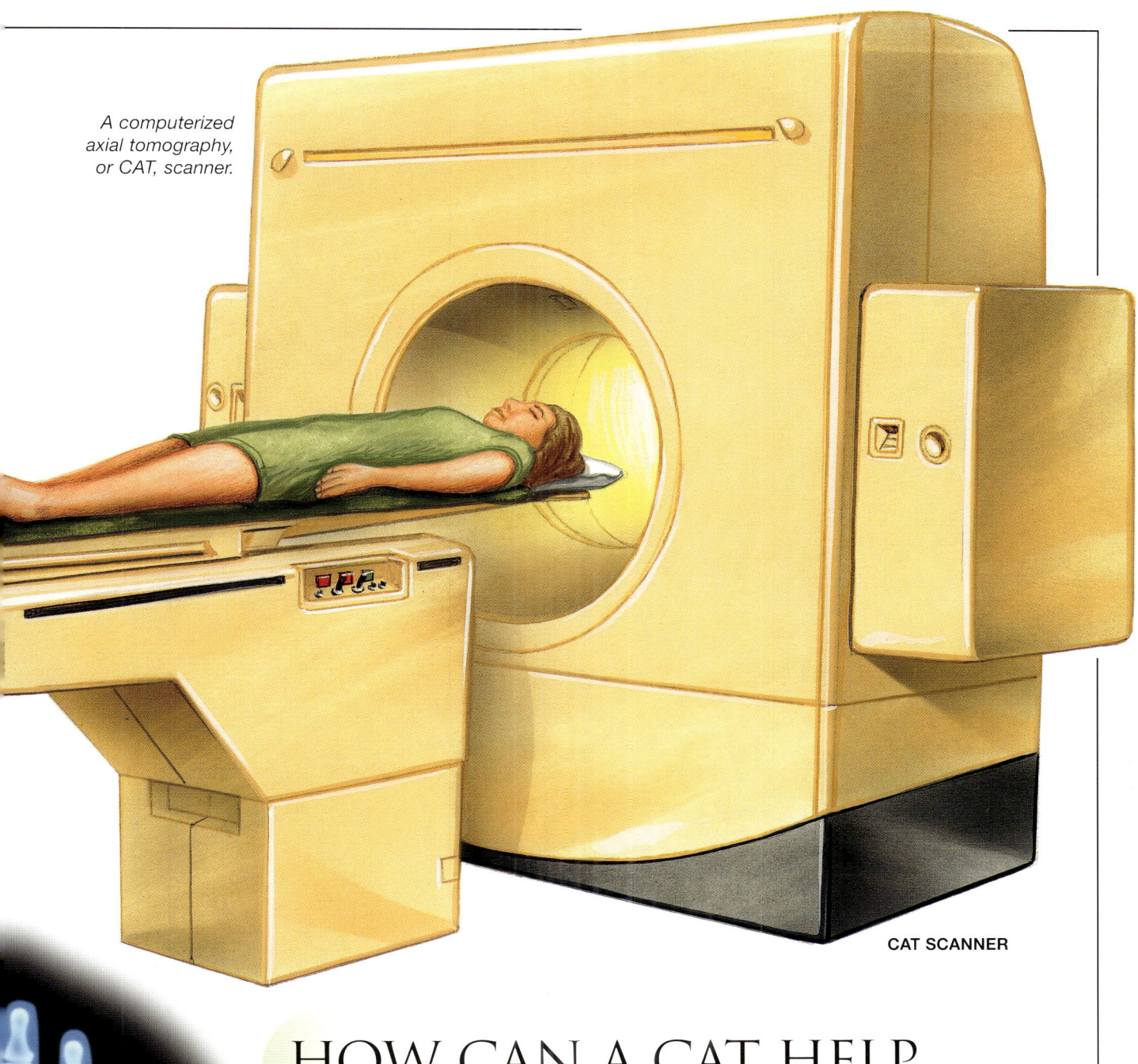

A computerized axial tomography, or CAT, scanner.

CAT SCANNER

HOW CAN A CAT HELP YOU IN HOSPITAL?

Doctors use a CAT (Computerized Axial Tomography) scan to build up a three-dimensional "map" of a patient's body. The patient lies on a table inside a circular scanning machine, and X-rays are passed through their body from many different angles. Computers then convert the readings into a detailed picture. CAT scans can detect such things as tumors and blood clots.

WHAT IS A SPHYGMOMANOMETER?

A sphygmomanometer is a machine used to read blood pressure. It has an inflatable cuff, a pump, and a gauge filled with mercury. A nurse wraps the cuff around the patient's upper arm and uses the pump to inflate the cuff until it is tight enough to stop the blood flowing to the lower arm. Air is then released until the blood flows again, at which point a pressure reading can be taken from the gauge.

WHICH COUNTRY PRODUCED THE FIRST GUIDED MISSILE?

During the Second World War, Germany developed two types of guided missile which they used mostly against London and the Belgian city of Antwerp. These terrifying war machines were called the V-1 and V-2, but were known as doodlebugs.

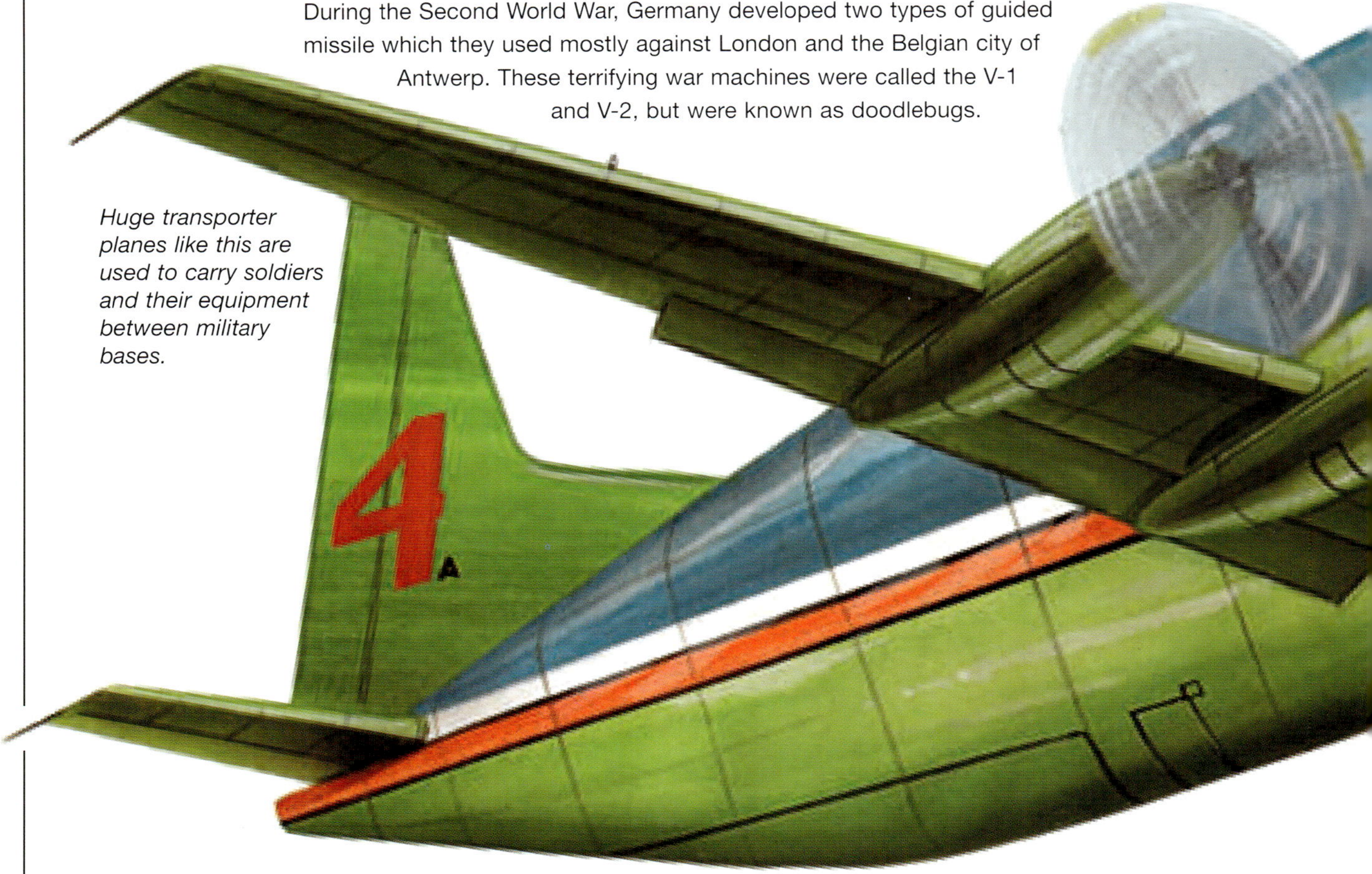

Huge transporter planes like this are used to carry soldiers and their equipment between military bases.

WHEN DID THE TANK BECOME A WAR MACHINE?

Leonardo da Vinci sketched an idea for a tank over 500 years ago. But the tank was first used in warfare during the First World War, at the Battle of the Somme in 1916. It was a lozenge shape, and the armour was only about ¼ in thick so it did not give the crew of eight much protection. During development, the British called their new war machines "water tanks" to conceal their purpose from enemy spies.

An American Abrams M-i battle tank.

WHY IS A JEEP CALLED A JEEP?

In 1941, the US government gave motor manufacturers 75 days to come up with a new "general purpose" vehicle for the military. The contract was won by Willys-Overland Motors, who built over 600,000 of the new "jeeps" between 1941 and 1945. The name jeep came from the initials GP— for "general purpose."

WHAT IS RADAR?

Radar stands for radio detection and ranging, and works by sending out radio waves then measuring how long it takes for them to bounce back. In this way, radar can track objects which are thousands of miles away.

HOW CAN A WAR MACHINE BECOME INVISIBLE?

The US Air Force's B-2 "stealth" bomber airplane has a sleek shape like a wing to deflect radio waves, and is painted with a special coating which absorbs them. So, it is difficult to detect by radar, and becomes "invisible" on a radar screen.

WHAT IS A "SMART BOMB?"

Through history most bombs and missiles have been "dumb"—they just fly in the direction in which they are fired. Computers on board modern bombs and missiles make them "smart." They can change course, hunt for targets, and decide whether or not to attack them.

WHO INVENTED THE MACHINE GUN?

There were many attempts to invent a gun that would fire rapidly and without the need to pull the trigger more than once. The first successful machine gun was designed by Richard J. Gatling in 1362. His "Gatling gun" had a revolving cylinder with ten parallel barrels. It fired 1,200 shots a minute and was soon used by every major army in the world. An improved, fully automatic machine gun was patented in 1884 by Sir Hiram Maxim.

WHY DO GUNS "RECOIL?"

They are obeying the same law of physics— every action has an equal and opposite reaction—as jet planes. When a bullet leaves the barrel in one direction, the gun moves or "recoils" the other way.

WHO INVENTED THE TELEPHONE?

The American Alexander Graham Bell invented the first working telephone. The telegraph, a machine which could transmit sounds, had already been invented, but Bell's was the first machine to transmit speech. Bell applied for a patent for his new invention in 1876. Another inventor, Elisha Gray, applied for a similar patent for his own invention only two hours later. If only he could have phoned!

WAS THE TELEGRAPH A BRITISH OR AMERICAN INVENTION?

It was a British invention, but the American version became more popular. In 1837, the British inventors Charles Wheatstone and William Cooke invented the five-needle telegraph. In 1841, Samuel Morse first demonstrated his own system, which used the famous "dot and dash" code.

Alexander Graham Bell would probably not recognize this modern mobile as a telephone.

WHICH MACHINE DID PLASTIC HELP?

The rise of the telephone came at the same time as the development of a new material called plastic. The first kind of plastic to be made was called Bakelite. It allowed telephones to be mass-produced rather than made by hand.

WHEN WAS THE FIRST TELEGRAPH CABLE LAID UNDER THE ATLANTIC?

The first Atlantic cable was laid in August 1858, but by September a fault had developed. In July 1866, the ship Great Eastern set off from England to the USA and successfully connected the two countries with nearly 2,800 miles of cable.

HOW DO MOBILE TELEPHONES COMMUNICATE?

Mobile telephones are actually radio transmitters and receivers. A cellular phone network is divided into geographical areas known as cells. Inside each cell is an antenna that keeps track of all mobile telephones in that cell. When one is dialled, the call is sent to its last known location. If it is not there, then neighboring cells are checked.

MOBILE TELEPHONE

HOW DID THE COLD WAR CREATE THE INTERNET?

During the 1960s, the US military were looking for ways to protect information on computers in the event of a nuclear attack. In 1969 they started the ARPAnet project, which linked all the computers in the US Defense Department around the country. This ARPAnet network eventually grew into the worldwide network of computers we know as the Internet.

WHO WAS THE FIRST CRIMINAL TO GET CAUGHT BY RADIO?

In 1910, Dr Harley Crippen murdered his wife and tried to escape to Canada with his mistress. A description of Crippen was transmitted to the ship by radio, and the captain recognized him among his passengers. He radioed the Canadian police who were waiting when the ship arrived.

All around the world, hundreds of millions of people use the Internet for work, education, and leisure.

HOW DOES A FAX MACHINE WORK?

When a document is fed into a fax machine, a scanner divides the picture into tiny black or white squares called pels. These are sent down the telephone line as a series of electrical signals. A black pel means the signal is on, a white pel means it is off. These electric signals can be used to reconstruct and print the original picture.

COMPUTER CONNECTED TO THE INTERNET

WHICH RADIO NEEDS NO ELECTRICITY TO WORK?

In 1991, Trevor Baylis invented the clockwork radio. This wonderful machine enables people without a supply of electricity to listen to radio programs. Over 20,000 a month are made in a factory in South Africa.

HOW DOES A MACHINE HELP ASTRONAUTS SPACE WALK?

When an astronaut leaves a spacecraft and goes "space walking" he or she can move in zero gravity by wearing a Manned Maneuvering Unit (MMU). This machine is attached to the back of a spacesuit. It has 24 tiny gas jets on it, which can be fired at different times to move the astronaut in any direction. Because each MMU costs about $9 million, only three have been built.

WHAT IS A "GEOSTATIONARY" SATELLITE?

Many communication and weather satellites orbit at about 22,370 miles above the Earth, and travel at the same speed and in the same direction as the Earth. This makes them appear to stand still. Satellites which remain above the same point on Earth in this way are called "geostationary."

WHERE DO SATELLITES GET THEIR ENERGY FROM?

Once a satellite is in space it needs electricity to work. This electricity comes from solar cells in large panels on the sides of the satellite. These are pointed at the Sun, and solar energy is converted into electricity and stored in batteries.

An astronaut wearing an MMU during a space walk.

WHICH PLANET WAS THE FIRST TO BE EXPLORED BY SATELLITE?

The first satellite to fly past another planet was the American *Mariner 2* which passed by Venus on December 14, 1962. The Soviet Union's *Venera 9* landed on Venus 13 years later and provided close-up photographs of the surface.

WHAT WAS THE LARGEST SPACE ROCKET?

The American rocket *Saturn V* dwarfs all other rockets. It flew from 1967 to 1973 as part of the Apollo moon missions. It was 363 feet high, weighed over 2000 tons, and could carry 150 tons in space.

WHICH MACHINES ARE CARRYING MESSAGES FOR ALIENS?

Pioneer and *Voyager* spacecraft are set to leave our solar system, carrying objects chosen to show life on Earth to any aliens they meet. The Voyagers have a gold-plated record which plays greetings in 60 languages and the sounds of birds and whales.

WHAT WAS THE FIRST MACHINE IN SPACE?

The first machine in space was *Sputnik I* which was launched by the Soviet Union on October 4, 1957. It was a test satellite and contained a radio beacon and a thermometer. Its launching was a great surprise to many people in the West and marked the start of the "space race" between the USA and the Soviet Union. The second Sputnik was launched one month later and carried the first living thing into space—a dog called Laika.

SPACE SHUTTLE

The outside of each Space Shuttle is covered with thousands of heat-resistant tiles.

HOW SMALL WILL MACHINES BE IN THE FUTURE?

Scientists and engineers working in the field of "nanotechnology" are looking for ways to make machines as small as possible, so they can work with individual atoms and molecules. Scientists will soon be building machines 100 nanometers in length. That is about the same size as a common cold virus. Tiny nanorobots will one day be sent into the bloodstream to remove or repair damaged tissue in the human body.

In the near future, small handheld machines may act as a phone, TV, video player, computer, and e-mail machine in one.

HOW WILL WE COMMUNICATE IN THE FUTURE?

The number of people buying a mobile phone is rising every week. The latest mobile phones can send and receive e-mail, and soon they will display video pictures, so that people can look at each other while they speak.

WILL ENTERTAINMENT CHANGE MUCH?

The rise of digital technology means that people will have a much greater choice of television programs to watch. There will be hundreds more channels to choose from, and viewers will be able to choose their own programs and decide when to watch them. Soccer fans can already choose which camera to watch a game from.

A surgeon using a virtual reality device to train in eye surgery.

WHO WILL DO THE HOUSEWORK?

Many household machines will become "intelligent," and will be able to communicate with each other and with their owners. Refrigerators will be able to tell when milk supplies are low and order more. Robots can already understand spoken commands, and in the future will do housework without being given instructions.

WHAT IS VIRTUAL REALITY?

Virtual reality is a computer-generated, three-dimensional world, which seems real to people using it. It can make computer games very realistic. In the future, people will experience the thrill of dangerous activities such as bungee-jumping without being exposed to any danger. Special suits will imitate the sensation on the skin of wind or water.

HOW WILL MACHINES TRAVEL IN THE FUTURE?

The amount of oil available to power the many machines we use for travel will soon become scarce and run out. Vehicles of the future will have to become very fuel efficient and will need to find new sources of power. These might include hydrogen, alcohol, or solar power. Trains of the future might be powered by a high-strength magnetic field. The Japanese are already trying to develop such "maglev" trains.

WHAT USE ARE VIRTUAL REALITY MACHINES TO SURGEONS?

Surgeons use virtual reality today to help with their training. One day it will help surgeons to perform complex operations even though they are thousands of miles away from the patient. The surgeon will look into a mask which will show the body of the patient, and wear gloves which move a robotic arm over the patient.

The screen shows the instructor what the surgeon can see in his virtual reality headset.

SECTION SIX

PLANT LIFE

The leaf is made up of cells. The dark green spots contain chlorophyll.

LEAF WITH MAGNIFIED SECTION

WHY ARE MOST PLANTS GREEN?

Most plants are green because they contain the green pigment chlorophyll in their stems and leaves. Sometimes the green pigment is masked by other colors, such as red. This means that not all plants that contain chlorophyll look green.

HOW DO GREEN PLANTS FEED?

Green plants make their own food in a process called photosynthesis. Chlorophyll, the green pigment in plants, helps to trap energy from the Sun. Plants use this energy to convert water and carbon dioxide into sugars and starch. They get the water and carbon dioxide from the soil and the air.

HOW DOES A PARASITIC PLANT FEED?

Parasitic plants do not need to make their own food, and many are not green. Instead, they grow into the tissues of another plant, called the host, and tap into its food and water transport system, taking all the nourishment they need from its sap.

HOW DO PLANTS TAKE IN WATER?

Plants use their extensive root systems to take in water from the ground. Each root branches into a network of rootlets, which in turn bear root hairs. Water passes into the root across the cell walls of millions of tiny root hairs.

THE DEVELOPMENT OF A POPPY FLOWER

The bud turns up toward the Sun and the petals open further.

The bud begins to open in the warm sunshine.

The poppy flower is ready to burst from its bud.

HOW DOES A VENUS FLY-TRAP CATCH ITS PREY?

The fly-trap is a carnivorous (meat-eating) plant that catches insects and other small animals. The trap is a flattened, hinged pad at the end of each leaf, fringed with bristles. When an insect lands on the pad and touches one of the sensitive hairs growing there, the trap is sprung and closes over the insect, and the bristles interlock to prevent its escape.

HOW FAST DOES SAP FLOW THROUGH A TREE?

In warm conditions, with a plentiful supply of water to the roots, and on a breezy day, sap may flow through a tree as fast as 40 inches every hour.

WHAT DOES A PLANT NEED TO GROW?

Plants need water, mineral salts, and foods such as carbohydrates. Green plants make their own foods, while other plants may take in food from decaying plants or animals, or direct from other living plants.

WHAT MAKES A SEED GROW?

To grow, a seed needs moisture, warmth, and air. Some seeds can only germinate (begin to grow) if they have first been in the low temperatures of winter. The seeds of some plants can lie dormant (inactive) for years before germinating.

The fruit capsule, containing the ripened seeds, is fully developed. The seeds can be shaken by the wind through the holes at the top.

The petals have fallen off, leaving the seed capsule.

The poppy is now fully open with its petals unfurled.

HOW MUCH SUGAR DOES PHOTOSYNTHESIS MAKE IN A YEAR?

Plants turn the sugar they make by the process of photosynthesis into other chemical compounds that they need for growth and development. They also use sugar to provide energy to run the reactions that take place in their cells. Some scientists have estimated that the total mass of green plants alive in the entire world make more than 150,000 million tons of sugar every year by their photosynthesis.

HOW DOES A FLOWER FORM SO QUICKLY?

When a flower opens out from a bud, it may appear like magic in just a day or even a few hours. This is possible because the flower is already formed in miniature inside the bud, just waiting to open out. If you cut open a flower bud you will see that all the flower's parts are there inside the bud. The bud opens as its cells take in water and grow. Many flowers form their buds in the fall, winter, or early spring, ready to open quickly in the warmer, sunnier weather of spring or early summer.

WHY DO SHOOTS GROW UPWARD?

Most shoots grow upward, toward the sunlight. The growing tip of the shoot can detect the direction of the light, and chemicals are released that make it grow more on the lower or darker side, thus turning the shoot upward.

WHY DO ROOTS GROW DOWNWARDS?

Roots grow downward because they can detect the pull of gravity. The root responds to gravity by releasing chemicals that cause more growth on the upper side, thus turning the root downward.

HOW MUCH POLLEN DO FLOWERS MAKE?

Flowers can produce enormous quantities of pollen. Some American ragweeds can produce 1,500 million pollen grains in an hour. Thus they can release 18,000 million grains of pollen in one day. The American ragweed is a major cause of hay fever, which is bad news for sufferers: US estimates put ragweed pollen production at a staggering 8 tons a week over a single square mile!

STIGMA

STAMEN

A FLOWER IN CROSS-SECTION

STYLE

OVARY

OVULE

FLOWER STALK

WHY DO FLOWERS OPEN IN SPRING/SUMMER?

In temperate regions many flowers open in spring or summer because this is the best time of year to attract insect pollinators. Ideally, the flowers open as early as possible in the season so that they can use the warm summer to grow and develop their seeds.

WHICH FLOWERS ARE POLLINATED BY MAMMALS?

The flowers of the African baobab tree are pollinated by bushbabies and bats. Those of the saguaro, or giant cactus, in the southwestern USA and Mexico, are pollinated by birds in the day, and bats at night.

HOW ARE FLOWERS POLLINATED?

Pollination is an important part of sexual reproduction in plants. The pollen, containing the male sex cells, fertilizes the ovules, which are the female sex cells. This can happen in several different ways. The flowers of many trees release masses of tiny pollen grains into the air, and the breeze takes some to their destination. Many water plants produce pollen that floats downstream. Many flowers have evolved their structure, colors, and scent to attract animals to pollinate them. The animal lands on the flower to feed from its nectar, gets showered with pollen, then moves off, transporting the pollen to the next flower it visits. Insects such as bees, wasps, and butterflies often pollinate flowers in this way, but some (mainly tropical) flowers are pollinated by birds, bats, and even small mammals.

HOW MANY SEEDS CAN A PLANT PRODUCE?

In the tropical forests of Central and South America, a single trumpet tree produces 900,000 tiny seeds. These end up in the soil and germinate when there is a gap in the canopy (the roof of the forest).

WHY ARE MANY SEEDS POISONOUS?

Many mammals and birds eat seeds. Some plants have seeds that are poisonous to mammals and birds, which prevents them being eaten. Poisonous seeds are often brightly colored so the seed-eaters quickly learn to spot them and avoid them.

CAN PLANTS REPRODUCE WITHOUT SEEDS?

Some plants, such as mosses, liverworts, and ferns, do not produce seeds. Instead, they spread by dispersing spores. But even among seeding plants reproduction without seeds is possible. Many plants can reproduce vegetatively by sending out runners or splitting off from bulbs, or swollen stems.

HOW ARE SEEDS DISPERSED?

Many seeds are dispersed by animals. Birds eat berries and pass out the tougher seeds unharmed in their droppings. Some fruit capsules have hooks that catch in animal fur and are transported that way, eventually falling free in another spot. Orchids have microscopic seeds that are dispersed by air currents. Some heavier seeds can also travel by air. The sycamore has "helicopter" wings, and dandelion seeds have feathery plumes. Many legumes have pods that split open as they ripen and dry, flinging out the seeds in the process.

WHERE DO SEEDS DEVELOP?

Each ovule is destined to become a seed, and develops inside the ovary of the flower. An ovule consists of the zygote, or fertilized egg, surrounded by the endosperm, the seed's initial food store.

WHICH PLANTS HAVE THE SMALLEST SEEDS?

Orchids produce the smallest seeds. They are microscopic and released in large numbers, to drift invisibly through the air. In some orchids, just 1 gram contains over 990 million seeds.

A STRAWBERRY PLANT

Strawberries reproduce vegetatively by sending out runners. The plantlet develops at the end of the runner and eventually grows into a separate plant.

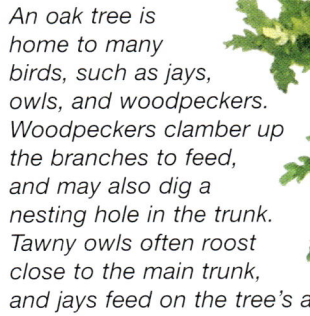

An oak tree is home to many birds, such as jays, owls, and woodpeckers. Woodpeckers clamber up the branches to feed, and may also dig a nesting hole in the trunk. Tawny owls often roost close to the main trunk, and jays feed on the tree's acorns.

WHAT LIVES IN A TREE?

Trees provide homes for countless animals, and also for other plants. The tree's leaves are eaten by the caterpillars of moths and butterflies and other insects, and many species of beetle lay their eggs in the tree's bark. Birds select a fork in a branch to build a nest, or use a natural hole in the trunk, and wild bees may also choose to nest inside a hollow tree. Many mammals are also tree dwellers, including squirrels, monkeys, sloths, bats, and koalas. In moist climates, other plants—especially mosses and ferns, and in the tropics orchids and bromeliads—can grow directly on the tree, in hollows where leaf litter gathers; they are known as epiphytes.

WHAT IS THE NITROGEN CYCLE?

Bacteria in the soil use nitrogen from the air and turn it into a form that plants can use. Plants then use the nitrogen in their cells to make many complex compounds. When animals eat plants (or other animals that have eaten plants) they continue the cycle. The nitrogen returns to the soil in the droppings of animals or from the decaying bodies of plants and animals.

HOW ARE PLANTS USED TO CLEAN UP SEWAGE?

Sewage works use tiny algae and other microscopic organisms in their filter beds. The sewage beds contain layers of gravel and sand, which support the growth of millions of algae. These algae and other organisms feed on the pollutants in the water and help to make it clean.

HOW DO FORESTS HELP IMPROVE THE AIR?

Forests help to preserve the quality of the air we breathe. They do this by releasing huge quantities of water vapor and oxygen into the atmosphere. Plants also absorb carbon dioxide, and help prevent this gas from building up to damaging levels.

HOW DO PLANTS RECYCLE WATER?

Plants help to return water to the air through the process of transpiration. This is when water evaporates from the stems and leaves of plants. Water enters the plant through its roots. A column of water moves up through the plant, from the roots right through the trunk or stem, into the leaves.

WILDLIFE IN AN OAK TREE

WHAT HAPPENS TO ALL THE LEAVES THAT FALL?

Huge quantities of leaves fall each season from forest trees, but they do not build up on the woodland floor from year to year. The dead leaves are attacked—for example by fungi and bacteria—and break down, gradually becoming part of the soil. The leaves are also eaten by many animals, including worms, insects, slugs, snails, millipedes, and woodlice.

Many fungi, such as these bracket fungi, may grow from the tree's trunk.

HOW DO PLANTS COLONIZE BARE GROUND?

Some plants can quickly colonize bare soil. They do this by germinating rapidly from lightweight wind-blown seeds. Some colonizing plants spread by putting out shoots called runners, which split off, becoming new plants.

HOW DO PLANTS MAKE THE SOIL MORE FERTILE?

When plants die, they decompose, releasing the chemicals in their tissues into the surrounding soil. The mixture of rotting leaves and other plant material in the soil is called humus, and this makes the soil more fertile.

HOW DO PLANTS HELP US RECLAIM LAND?

Several types of grass, including marram, can be planted on coastal dunes. Their roots anchor the sand and help to stop it blowing away. The plants also build up a layer of humus (decayed plant matter), enriching the developing soil. Plants can even begin to reclaim land contaminated by industrial poisons. Some species have evolved forms that can tolerate toxic substances. They gradually improve the fertility and build up the soil so that other plants can grow there too.

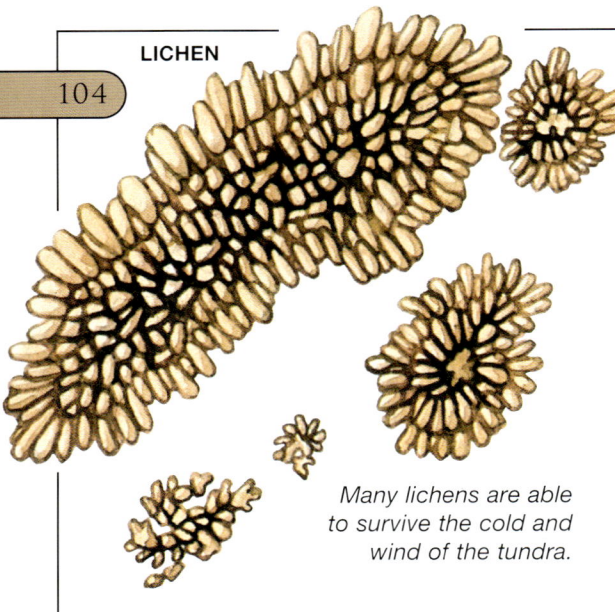

Many lichens are able to survive the cold and wind of the tundra.

WHAT IS THE TUNDRA LIKE?

The most striking feature of the tundra is its total lack of trees. There is not enough warmth for woody plants to grow unless they are very small. The dominant plants are grasses and sedges, mosses and lichens, with shrubs such as heathers, and dwarf willows and birches. There are also many flowers such as saxifrages, avens, and Arctic poppies.

WHAT IS THE MOST NORTHERLY FLOWER?

A species of poppy has been found further north than any other flower—at 83°N, or on a level with the north of Greenland.

WHY ARE MANY TUNDRA FLOWERS WHITE OR YELLOW?

Most tundra flowers are pollinated by insects. However, there are relatively few bees this far north, and the main pollinators are flies. Flies cannot distinguish colors like bees can, so the flowers do not need to be so colorful.

WHAT IS PERMAFROST?

Even where the surface soil in the Arctic thaws in the summer, further down it is permanently frozen. This icy layer is known as the permafrost. Because the ice prevents rain water seeping further down, the surface can be wet.

WHERE IS THE TUNDRA?

The tundra lies north of the coniferous forest belt, in a band roughly following the Arctic Circle. It covers a huge area of land—about 10 million square miles, from Alaska, through Canada, Greenland, Iceland, across to North Norway and Sweden and on around the Arctic coast of Siberia. Only a small area of the Antarctic has similar conditions—the peninsula reaching north toward the tip of South America.

HOW DO SOME POLAR PLANTS MELT THE SNOW?

Several Arctic and mountain plants that survive under the snow have dark colored leaves and stems. When the Sun begins to shine, they absorb the heat and melt the snow around them.

WHY DO MANY ARCTIC PLANTS HAVE SWOLLEN ROOTS?

Many Arctic plants have swollen roots or underground stems. They contain food reserves in readiness for a quick spurt of growth in the following summer.

WHY ARE THERE MORE PLANTS IN THE ARCTIC?

The Arctic is surrounded by land masses—from Canada and Greenland to northern Europe and Siberia, with many islands. These offer many open habitats for plant growth, especially in the summer. About 900 species are native to the Arctic tundra.

WHY ARE THERE SO FEW PLANTS IN THE ANTARCTIC?

Most of Antarctica is covered with snow and ice all year. Only the Antarctic Peninsula has habitats where plants can survive, because it is warmed by the sea. Only two kinds of flowering plant—a hair-grass and a cushion plant—are native to Antarctica.

WHY ARE MANY ARCTIC SHRUBS EVERGREEN?

Many Arctic shrubs keep some or all of their leaves throughout the winter. Leaves formed in late summer stay on the plant, often protected by dead leaves formed earlier. Then as soon as the spring returns, the green leaves can begin to photosynthesize.

The plants of the Arctic include pretty flowers such as the Arctic poppy, low-growing cushion plants, and tiny trees such as dwarf birch and willow.

ARCTIC SCENE

WHY DO MOST WATER PLANTS GROW ONLY IN SHALLOW WATER?

Most plants need to root themselves in the soil, even if they live mainly submerged in the water. In deep water there is not enough sunlight for plants to grow successfully.

HOW ARE WETLANDS DAMAGED?

When soil is drained, or too much water is pumped from the land nearby, wetlands suffer as the water-table is lowered. Wetlands are easily damaged by pollution as well. Sewage and chemicals released from factories easily find their way into streams and rivers, where they can upset the balance of nature and poison the wildlife.

HOW DOES THE BLADDERWORT FEED?

Bladderwort is a carnivorous plant found in boggy pools. The underwater stems develop small bladders, each with a trigger. When a small animal, such as a water flea, bumps into the trigger, the bladder springs open, sucking in the animal with the in-rushing water.

HOW DO WATER PLANTS GET THEIR FLOWERS POLLINATED?

Even though their growth is mainly below the surface, most water plants hold their flowers above the water, for pollination by the wind or by insects. Some, like the water starwort, have water-resistant floating pollen that drifts to the female flowers.

HOW DO WATER PLANTS STAY AFLOAT?

Some water plants stay afloat because their tissues contain chambers of air, making their stems and leaves buoyant. Others, such as water lilies, have flat, rounded leaves that sit boat-like on the water surface. They may also have waxy leaves, which repel the water and help to keep the leaves afloat, or up-curved rims to the leaves. Some combine wax with hairs so that the leaves are unwettable. Duckweeds are so small and light that the surface tension of the water is enough to keep them afloat, and the water hyacinth has inflated leaf-bases that act as floats.

HOW DO RIVER PLANTS COPE WITH THE CURRENT?

Few plants can grow in the current of fast rivers, except for tiny algae encrusting stones on the riverbed. But in the eddies and slower currents of the riverbank they can gain a roothold. River plants have to anchor themselves firmly with roots. They then tend to grow narrow ribbon- or strap-like leaves that offer little resistance to the water flow. Others, like water milfoil, have finely divided, feathery leaves, for the same reason. Water crowfoot sends up thin, flexible stems that bend and sway in the current.

WHY DO SOME LAKES HAVE VERY FEW PLANTS?

Lakes vary in the chemical composition of the water that they contain. Some lakes, such as those draining from lime-rich soils, are very fertile and can support a lot of plants. Others, especially those whose water is acid (as in granite areas), are poor in nutrients and therefore poor in plant life.

HOW DOES A LAKE TURN INTO LAND?

Over time, a lake will gradually turn into dry land by a process called succession. Slowly, the remains of the plants growing in the shallows accumulate, making the water more and more shallow. Eventually, the edges of the lake dry out and land plants can establish themselves.

WHAT FOOD PLANTS COME FROM WETLANDS?

The most important wetland crop is rice, which is grown in many parts of the world, notably India and China. Rice grows best in special flooded fields, called paddies. Another aquatic grass crop is Canadian wild rice, a traditional food of native Americans, and now a popular specialty.

HOW DO WATER PLANTS DISPERSE THEIR FRUITS?

The running water of streams and rivers carries floating fruits along, and there is usually some water movement even in ponds and lakes. Many floating fruits have tough coats that stop them from germinating too soon, so that they can travel a good distance.

GENTIAN

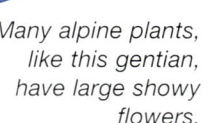

WHAT LIMITS PLANT GROWTH IN THE MOUNTAINS?

The climate changes as the land rises from valley to mountain, it gets colder with increased height, and also windier. There is also usually much less level ground in the mountains, and the soils are thinner. Other factors that influence plant growth are the amount of sunshine, and the pattern of snow and ice accumulation. In very exposed sites, the wind chills the ground and prevents snow from gathering, creating conditions that defeat even the hardiest of plants.

Many alpine plants, like this gentian, have large showy flowers.

HOW DO MOUNTAIN PLANTS ATTRACT POLLINATORS?

Many mountain plants have large, colorful flowers to attract the few insects that live there. Some, such as mountain avens, track the Sun to warm their flowers, which attracts insects to sunbathe there.

WHY DO DIFFERENT PLANTS GROW ON DIFFERENT SIDES OF A MOUNTAIN?

Different sides of a mountain have different climates. On the south side (or north side in the southern hemisphere), there is more sun and conditions are warmer, while on the other side the snow and ice stay on the ground much longer.

HOW DO PLANTS SURVIVE THE COLD?

Plants have evolved many different ways of surviving mountain conditions. Many grow close to the ground, in cushion-like shapes, which keeps them out of the wind. Some have thick, waxy, or hairy leaves to help insulate them.

HOW DO SOME MOUNTAIN PLANTS REPRODUCE WITHOUT FLOWERS?

Many mountain plants have dispensed with flowers because of the lack of insects to pollinate them, and reproduce vegetatively instead. Thus some mountain grasses grow miniature plants where the flowers should be—these drop off and grow into new plants.

WHY IS IT COLDER IN THE MOUNTAINS?

The Sun heats the ground and this heat is trapped close to the ground by the Earth's atmosphere. As you go up a mountain, and rise above the zone in which the heat is held, the atmosphere gets thinner and the air gets colder. It falls about 34°F for every 495 feet in height.

ALPINE FLOWERS

These alpine flowers are growing in a natural rock garden.

HOW CAN PLANTS SURVIVE THE SNOW AND ICE?

Few plants can survive being completely frozen, but many can thrive under the snow. Snow acts like a blanket to keep the freezing ice and wind at bay, and saves the plants from being killed. Alpine grasses stay alive and green under the snow, ready to grow again as soon as it melts.

WHY ARE ALPINE FLOWERS SO POPULAR IN GARDENS?

Many mountain plants, such as gentians and saxifrages, are known as alpines—because they come from the Alps. They are popular for their bright flowers, and also because they tend to grow well even in poor conditions, such as on a rock garden.

WHAT IS THE TREE LINE?

Trees cannot grow all the way up a mountain, and the highest level for them is known as the tree line. This varies according to the local climate of the region, but is around 9,250 feet in the Alps. Trees at this level grow slowly and are often stunted.

HOW DOES THE PLANT LIFE CHANGE AS YOU GO UP A MOUNTAIN?

Conditions generally get harsher, the higher you go up a mountain, and the plant life reflects this. So, there may be temperate woodland in the lowlands, but as you climb, this changes, typically to coniferous woodland, then to mountain scrub, then to grassland, then again, with increasing height, to a tundra-like vegetation, and to rocky screes and snow-patches.

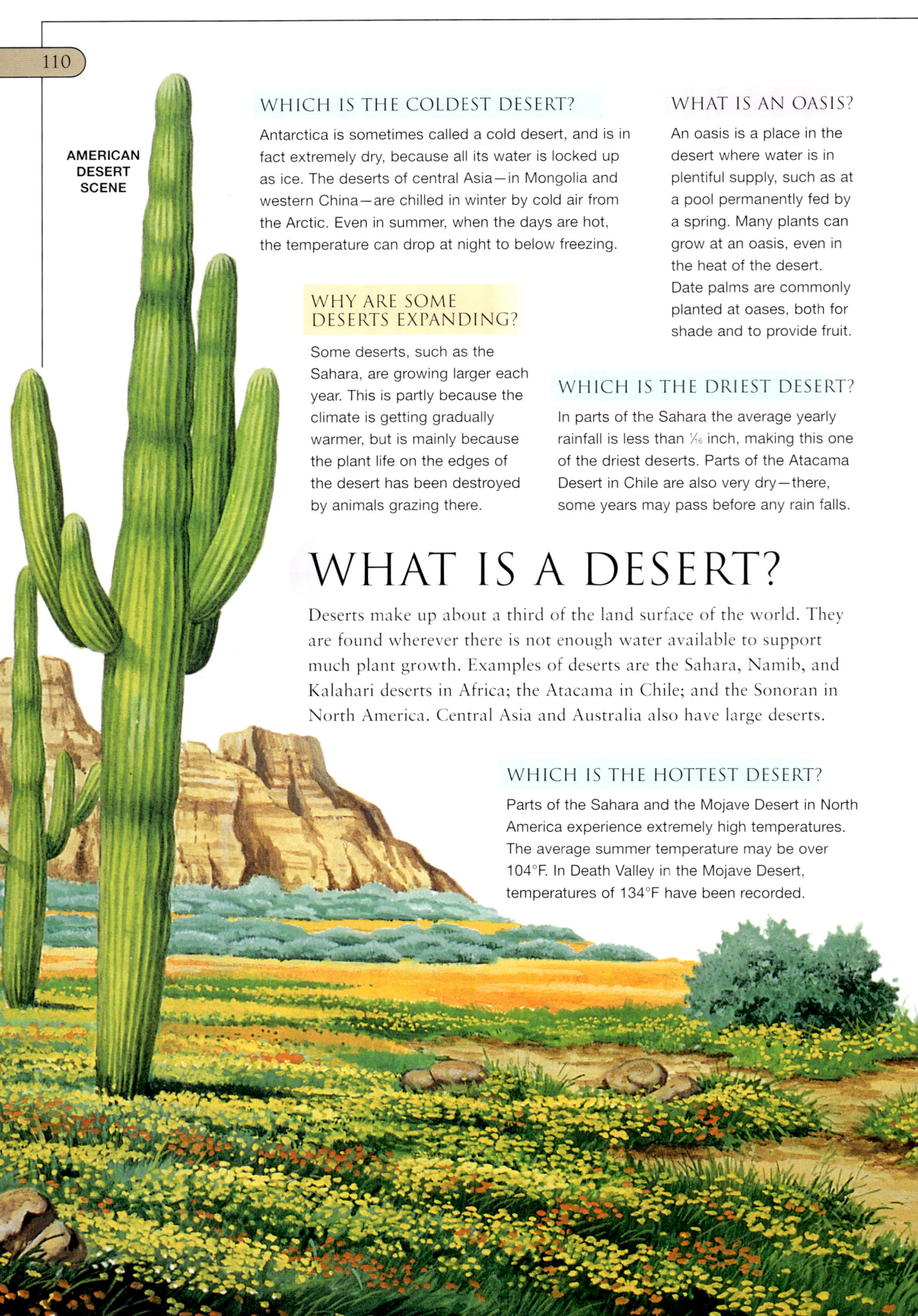

AMERICAN DESERT SCENE

WHICH IS THE COLDEST DESERT?

Antarctica is sometimes called a cold desert, and is in fact extremely dry, because all its water is locked up as ice. The deserts of central Asia—in Mongolia and western China—are chilled in winter by cold air from the Arctic. Even in summer, when the days are hot, the temperature can drop at night to below freezing.

WHY ARE SOME DESERTS EXPANDING?

Some deserts, such as the Sahara, are growing larger each year. This is partly because the climate is getting gradually warmer, but is mainly because the plant life on the edges of the desert has been destroyed by animals grazing there.

WHAT IS AN OASIS?

An oasis is a place in the desert where water is in plentiful supply, such as at a pool permanently fed by a spring. Many plants can grow at an oasis, even in the heat of the desert. Date palms are commonly planted at oases, both for shade and to provide fruit.

WHICH IS THE DRIEST DESERT?

In parts of the Sahara the average yearly rainfall is less than $\frac{1}{16}$ inch, making this one of the driest deserts. Parts of the Atacama Desert in Chile are also very dry—there, some years may pass before any rain falls.

WHAT IS A DESERT?

Deserts make up about a third of the land surface of the world. They are found wherever there is not enough water available to support much plant growth. Examples of deserts are the Sahara, Namib, and Kalahari deserts in Africa; the Atacama in Chile; and the Sonoran in North America. Central Asia and Australia also have large deserts.

WHICH IS THE HOTTEST DESERT?

Parts of the Sahara and the Mojave Desert in North America experience extremely high temperatures. The average summer temperature may be over 104°F. In Death Valley in the Mojave Desert, temperatures of 134°F have been recorded.

HOW DOES A CACTUS SURVIVE IN THE DESERT?

Cacti are special plants that live in the deserts of North and Central America. They have leafless, swollen stems that store water, and for this reason they are sometimes called succulents, as are similar fleshy plants of the African deserts. Since they lack leaves, they do not lose much water through transpiration. Most cacti are spiny, which probably protects them from being eaten by hungry (and thirsty) desert animals. Many cacti have furrowed stems. This allows them to expand with stored water after a rainstorm.

Cacti are protected by sharp spines. Many kinds also produce large colorful flowers.

A CACTUS IN FLOWER

HOW BIG IS THE LARGEST CACTUS?

The largest of all cacti is the giant cactus or saguaro, of the southwestern USA and Mexico. Saguaros can be 66 feet tall, and 2 feet thick. They can weigh as much as 12 tons and may live to be 200 years old.

WHAT LIVES IN A LARGE CACTUS?

Cacti are home to a variety of wildlife. Their flowers are visited by butterflies, moths, and hummingbirds. Holes in cactus stems provide nest sites for desert rodents, and also for birds like the tiny elf owl.

WHAT IS THE STRANGEST DESERT PLANT?

Welwitschia is probably the strangest desert plant of all. It lives for centuries, growing very slowly and producing just two twisted leathery leaves. It lives in the coastal deserts of Southwest Africa and gets its water mainly from sea-fog.

HOW DO "RESURRECTION" PLANTS SURVIVE THE DROUGHT?

When conditions get very dry, the leaves of resurrection plants shrivel up and turn brown. This cuts down the loss of water. When it rains, the leaves take in water, expand, and turn green again.

WHAT IS A JOSHUA TREE?

The Joshua tree grows in the Mojave Desert, California, USA. It grows very slowly and its leaves can last for 20 years. The leaves have fibers inside, and they are sometimes used to make paper.

HOW DEEP DO THE ROOTS OF DESERT PLANTS GO?

Some desert plants have very long roots that can tap into deep underground water sources. Mesquite roots often grow as deep as 10 metres (33 ft), and there are reports of roots over 50 metres (164 ft) below the surface.

The tallest plants in this American desert scene are the branched giant cacti or saguaros.

WHAT ARE THE MOST IMPORTANT FOOD CROPS?

Some 12,000 species of plant are known to have been used as food by people, and about 150 of these are in regular cultivation today. The most important crops are the cereals (grass-like crops)—wheat, rice, and maize (corn), followed by barley, sorghum, oats, millet, and rye. These form the basis of many people's diet throughout the world. Root crops are also widely grown. These include potatoes in temperate zones, and in tropical zones sweet potatoes, yams, and cassava or manioc. All these foods provide carbohydrates, while seeds of the pea family (known as pulses) are rich in protein. As well as peas and beans, these include soya beans, garbanzo beans, lentils, and peanuts.

Millet and sorghum are staple crops in much of Africa. Rice is the main food crop in Asia.

WHICH PLANTS GIVE US OIL?

The seeds of many plants are rich in oil, which they store as a source of food and energy. We extract oil from several of these plants, including olive, sunflower, corn (maize), soya bean, peanuts, oil-seed rape, sesame, and African oil palm.

WHERE DOES COFFEE COME FROM?

The coffee plant is a large shrub, and its berries are used to make coffee. The ripe berries are harvested, then dried to remove the flesh from the hard stones inside. These are the coffee "beans," which are then treated further, often being roasted.

Sunflower seeds and olives are crushed to produce oil.

WHICH PLANTS ARE USED TO MAKE SUGAR?

The main source of sugar is the sweet stems of the sugar cane, a tall grass that grows in tropical countries. In some temperate areas, including Europe, there are large crops of sugar beet. This plant stores sugar in its thickened roots. In some parts of the tropics, the sap of the sugar palm is made into sugar.

WHERE WERE POTATOES FIRST GROWN?

Potatoes grow wild in the Andes Mountains of South America and were first gathered as food by the native people of that region. All the many varieties grown today derive from that wild source.

WHAT IS BREADFRUIT?

Breadfruit is a tree, native to Polynesia, which grows to about 65 feet, and has large edible fruits. The fruits are up to 1 foot across and are cooked before being eaten as a vegetable.

The fresh young leaves of the tea bush are gathered to make tea.

TEA LEAVES

WHERE DID WHEAT COME FROM?

Wheat is one of the oldest known crops. It was probably first cultivated over 6,000 years ago in Mesopotamia—present-day Iraq—between the rivers Tigris and Euphrates. Many useful crop plants have their origin in the Middle East. Other examples are barley, oats and rye, peas and lentils, onions, olives, figs, apples, and pears.

HOW IS CHOCOLATE MADE?

The cocoa tree comes originally from the eastern Andes in South America. The fruits, called pods, develop on the sides of the trunk, and each pod contains about 20 to 30 seeds—the cocoa "beans." The beans must be fermented, roasted, and ground before they become cocoa powder, the raw material for making chocolate. Cocoa is now grown mainly in West Africa, and also in the Caribbean.

HOW IS TEA MADE?

Tea comes from the leaves of a species of camellia. This is planted on hillsides, especially in India and Sri Lanka, and in Indonesia, Japan, and China. The young leaf tips are harvested, dried, and then crushed to make tea.

A SELECTION OF FOOD PLANTS

WHICH TREES GIVE US A SWEET, SUGARY SYRUP?

The sugar maple has a sweet sap, which is harvested to make maple syrup. Most maple syrup comes from the province of Quebec, in Canada.

WHICH FRUITS ARE GROWN FOR FOOD?

Fruits of the temperate regions include apples, pears, grapes, plums, cherries, red and black currants, strawberries, raspberries, blackberries, and gooseberries. In warmer regions, a different selection is available, including citrus fruits such as oranges, grapefruits, lemons and tangerines, and also pineapples, melons, dates, figs, bananas, coconuts, mangoes, papayas, and guavas. Some fruits have a less sweet flavor, and are used as vegetables. Examples are tomatoes, avocados, and bell peppers. Fruits are very good for us. They contain energy-giving stores of natural sugar, as well as protein and vital vitamins. They also provide roughage to aid digestion.

Wheat, corn (maize), and barley are common in temperate regions.

SECTION SEVEN

EVERY LIVING CREATURE

Chimpanzees climb well and find much of their food in trees.

CHIMPANZEE

WHICH IS THE SMALLEST MONKEY?

The smallest monkey is the pygmy marmoset, which lives in South American rainforest. It is about 15 inches long, but half of this is tail, and it weighs only about 5 oz.

An adult chimpanzee is up to 33 inches long and does not have a tail.

DO CHIMPANZEES USE TOOLS?

Yes. The chimpanzee can get food by poking a stick into an ants' nest. It pulls out the stick and licks off the ants. It also uses stones to crack nuts, and it makes sponges from chewed leaves to mop up water or wipe its body.

DO CHIMPANZEES HUNT PREY?

Yes they do. Although fruit is the main food of chimpanzees, they also eat insects and hunt young animals such as monkeys. Male chimpanzees usually do the hunting. They work together in a group, some cutting a couple of animals out of the herd and driving them toward other chimps, who will make the kill. The rest of the troop then joins in to share the meat.

HOW MANY KINDS OF MONKEY ARE THERE?

About 133 species in three main groups. One group lives in Africa and Asia. The other two groups live in Central and South America.

DO CHIMPANZEES LIVE IN FAMILY GROUPS?

Yes, in very large families that may include between 25 and 100 animals, led by a dominant male. Each group has its own home range.

WHERE DO CHIMPANZEES LIVE?

Chimpanzees live in forest and grasslands in West and Central Africa. There is another less familiar chimpanzee species called the pygmy chimpanzee, or bonobo, which lives in rainforests in Zaire/Congo in Africa. It is slimmer and lighter than the common chimpanzee and spends more of its time in trees.

WHY DOES THE MONKEY HAVE A LONG TAIL?

To help it balance and control its movements as it leaps from branch to branch in the rainforest. The tails of South American monkeys are even more useful than those of their African and Asian relatives, because they are prehensile. A prehensile tail has special muscles that the monkey can use to twine round branches and help it climb—it's almost like having a fifth leg. The naked skin on the underside of the tail is ridged to improve grip.

WHAT IS AN APE?

Apes are the most advanced animals in the primate group, which also includes animals such as lemurs, bush babies, and monkeys. There are three families of apes. One includes all the different kinds of gibbons. The second contains the gorilla, chimpanzee, and orangutan and the third has one species only—humans.

DO ANY MONKEYS LIVE IN COLD PLACES?

Most monkeys are found in warm areas near to the equator, but some macaque monkeys live in cooler places. The rhesus macaque lives in the Himalayas as well as in parts of China and India, and the Japanese macaque survives freezing winters with the help of its thick coat

WHERE DO ORANGUTANS LIVE?

Orangutans live in Southeast Asia in the rainforests of Sumatra and Borneo. This ape has long reddish fur and spends most of its life in the trees. Fruit is its main food but the orangutan also eats leaves, insects, and even eggs and small animals. The orangutan is active during the day. At night it sleeps on the ground or in a nest of branches in the trees.

WHICH IS THE BIGGEST APE?

The gorilla—a fully grown male stands up to 5.5 feet tall and weighs as much as 400 lb. Gorillas live in rainforest in West and Central Africa. A family group contains an adult male, several females, and a number of young of different ages. The male, known as a silverback because of the white hair on his back, leads the group.

Gorillas usually move on all fours, leaning on the knuckles of their front limbs.

GORILLA FAMILY

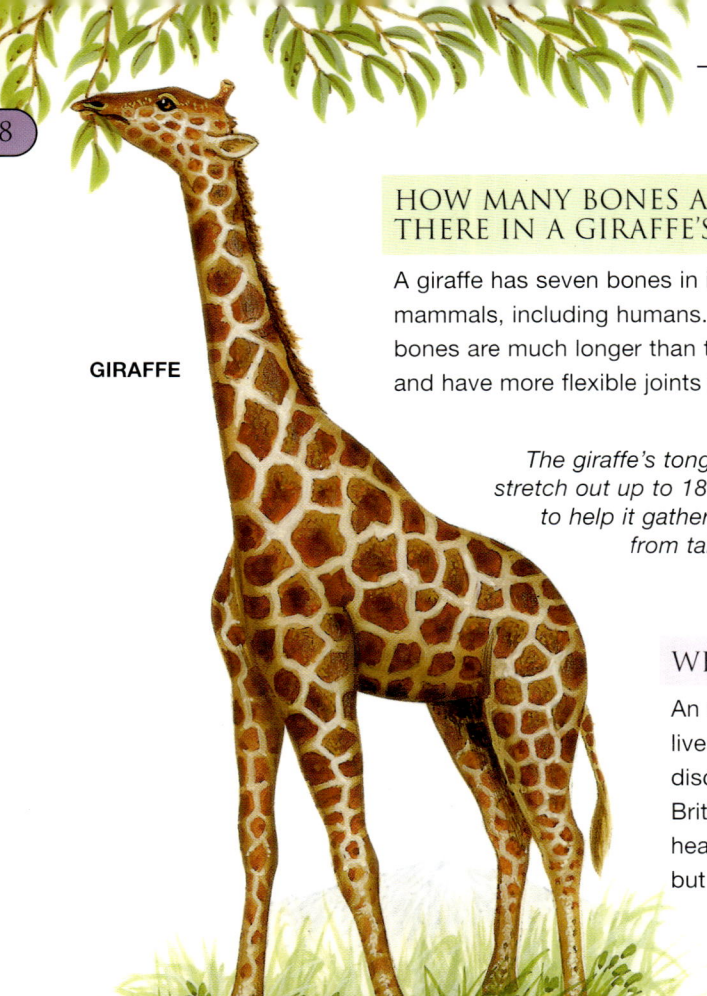

GIRAFFE

HOW MANY BONES ARE THERE IN A GIRAFFE'S NECK?

A giraffe has seven bones in its neck, just like other mammals, including humans. But the giraffe's neck bones are much longer than those of other animals, and have more flexible joints between them.

The giraffe's tongue can stretch out up to 18 inches to help it gather leaves from tall trees.

WHAT IS AN OKAPI?

An okapi is a relative of the giraffe that lives in the African rainforest. It was discovered as recently as 1901 by a British explorer. It has small horns on its head and a long tongue like a giraffe's—but it does not have a long neck.

ARE RHINOCEROSES FIERCE ANIMALS?

Despite their ferocious appearance and huge horns, rhinos are peaceful, plant-eating animals. But if threatened, a rhino will charge its enemy, galloping at high speed with its huge head held down ready to attack. Mothers defending their young can be particularly dangerous.

HOW TALL IS A GIRAFFE?

A male giraffe stands up to 18 feet tall to the tips of its horns. It has an extraordinarily long neck, and front legs that are longer than its back legs so the body slopes down toward the tail. The long neck allows it to feed on leaves high in trees that other animals cannot reach.

HOW BIG IS A BABY ELEPHANT?

A newborn baby elephant weighs up to 264 lb and stands up to 40 inches high. It feeds on its mother's milk for at least two years, by which time it may weigh more than 1,322 lb, and it may continue suckling for up to six years.

HOW CAN YOU TELL AN AFRICAN ELEPHANT FROM AN ASIAN ELEPHANT?

The African elephant is bigger and has larger ears and longer tusks. The head and body of the African elephant measures up to 24½ feet long. The Asian elephant measures up to 21 feet and has a more humped back. There is another difference at the end of the long trunk. The African elephant's trunk has two flexible finger-like lips, while the Asian animal's trunk has only one.

HOW LONG ARE AN ELEPHANT'S TUSKS?

An elephant's tusks grow throughout its life, so the oldest elephants have the longest tusks. An old male elephant may have tusks that measure up to 11 feet and weigh 264 lb.

The elephant flaps its huge ears to help keep itself cool.

The elephant's gray skin is up to 1¹⁄₂ inches thick and has a fine covering of hairs.

WHAT DO ELEPHANTS DO WITH THEIR TRUNKS?

The elephant's trunk is very useful. Without it, an elephant could not reach the ground to feed because its neck is so short. The trunk is also used for taking food from high in the trees and for breaking off branches. The elephant can smell with its trunk, pick up tiny objects, and gently caress its young. It drinks by sucking up water into its trunk and squirting it into its mouth. It also sprays water or dust over itself to clean its skin.

HOW MUCH DO ELEPHANTS EAT?

A fully grown elephant eats 220 to 440 lb of plant food a day, including grass, twigs, branches, leaves, flowers, and fruits.

MEERKATS ON GUARD

Meerkats thrive in the hostile Kalahari desert by working as a team. A group of adults watch out for predators while others are out hunting.

WHAT IS A MEERKAT?

A meerkat is a type of mongoose, which lives in Africa. Meerkats form large groups of up to 30 or more animals, which share the guarding of young and finding of food. Sentry meerkats often stand up on their hind legs to watch out for danger.

HOW MANY KINDS OF CAT ARE THERE?

There are about 35 species of wild cat, ranging from the tiger to the African wild cat, which is the main ancestor of domestic cats. Cats live in most parts of the world in every sort of habitat from tropical rainforest and desert to the icy lands of Siberia. There are no wild cats in Antarctica, Australia, or New Zealand.

WHICH CAT RUNS THE FASTEST?

The cheetah is the fastest running cat and one of the speediest of all animals over short distances. It has been timed running at 60 mph over 110 yards. Olympic sprinters can reach only about 30 mph.

WHAT DOES A MONGOOSE EAT?

The mongoose is a fast-moving little hunter. It will kill small creatures such as rats, mice, and frogs and will also take anything else it can find, including insects and birds' eggs. A mongoose will even tackle a large snake.

WHAT IS A SNOW LEOPARD?

The snow leopard is a big cat that lives in the Himalaya Mountains. It has a beautiful pale coat with dark markings, which has made it the target of fur poachers. Killing snow leopards for their fur is now illegal, but poaching still goes on.

WHY ARE LIONS UNLIKE OTHER CATS?

Most cats live alone. Lions live and hunt in a group called a pride. Tigers, cheetahs, and other big cats live alone, unless rearing young. A lion pride includes several adult males and a number of females, young lions and cubs. Living in a group means that there are always some adults to look after the cubs while others are off hunting. And working together, lions can bring down animals much larger than themselves, such as wildebeest and zebra.

WHERE DO JAGUARS LIVE?

Jaguars live in the forests of Central and South America. They are the largest South American cats and measure up to 6 feet long with a tail of up to 36 inches. Despite its size, the jaguar is a good climber and often clambers up a tree to watch for prey. It hunts other forest animals such as peccaries and capybaras as well as birds, turtles, and fish.

TIGER

WHY DO TIGERS HAVE STRIPES?

A tiger's stripes help it hide among grasses and leaves so it can surprise its prey. Tigers cannot run fast for long distances so they depend on being able to get close to their prey before making the final pounce. The stripes help to break up their outline and make them hard for prey to see.

WHAT IS A PANTHER?

A panther is simply a leopard with a black coat instead of spots. It is not a separate species of cat. Leopards live in Africa and Asia.

WHICH BIG CAT IS THE BIGGEST?

Tigers are the biggest of the big cats. They measure up to 10 feet long, including the tail, and weigh 550 lb or more. Tigers are becoming very rare. They live in parts of Asia, from snowy Siberia in the north to the tropical rainforests of Sumatra. There is only one species of tiger, but those in the north tend to be larger and have thicker, lighter colored fur than their relations further south. Tigers live alone, coming together only for mating. The female rears her cubs without the help of her mate. At first the cubs stay close to the den, but when they are about six months old they begin to go with their mother on hunts and learn how to find food for themselves.

The pattern of stripes on a tiger's skin is unique. No two tigers have quite the same pattern.

HOW DIFFERENT ARE OUR PET CATS FROM WILD CATS?

Pet cats and wild cats have exactly the same body structure and skeleton. Both rely heavily on smell for information about the world and they mark their territories by spraying urine or by rubbing the body against trees or other objects. All cats are meat-eaters and cannot live on a diet of plant foods.

IS A CIVET A KIND OF CAT?

No, civets belong to a separate family, which also includes mongooses, meerkats, and genets. Most civets live in tropical forests in Southeast Asia or Africa. They have a long, slender body, short legs, and a long tail.

WHICH WHALE DIVES THE DEEPEST?

The sperm whale dives to at least 3,300 feet below the surface of the sea and may go down to even greater depths when chasing giant squid to eat.

DO WHALES EVER COME TO LAND?

No, whales spend their whole lives in the sea. But they do breathe air and have to come to the surface regularly to take breaths.

HOW FAST DO WHALES SWIM?

Blue whales normally swim at about 5 mph but can move at speeds of up to 18 mph when disturbed. Some small whales, such as pilot whales and dolphins, may swim at more than 30 mph.

HOW DOES A BLUE WHALE FEED?

A blue whale filters small shrimp-like creatures called krill from the water. Hanging from the whale's upper jaw are lots of plates of a fringed bristly material called baleen. The whale opens its mouth, and water and krill flows in. The whale forces the water through the baleen with its tongue. The water flows out at the sides of the mouth, leaving the krill behind on the baleen for the whale to swallow.

DO HUMPBACK WHALES SING?

Yes, they do. They make a series of sounds, including high whistles and low rumbles, that may continue for hours. No one knows exactly why the humpback whale sings, but it may be to court a mate or to keep in touch with others in the group.

WHICH IS THE BIGGEST WHALE?

The blue whale is the largest whale, and also the largest mammal that has ever lived. It measures more than 100 feet long. It weighs at least 90 tons and the biggest blue whales may weigh more than twice this amount. Although it is so huge, the blue whale is not a fierce hunter. It eats tiny shrimp-like creatures called krill. It may gobble up as many as four million of these in a day.

HOW BIG IS A BABY BLUE WHALE?

A baby blue whale is about 23 feet long at birth and is the biggest baby in the animal kingdom. It weighs about 8 tons—that is more than a fully grown elephant.

BLUE WHALE

Dolphins leap out of the water as they swim and dive back in head first.

DOLPHINS

WHAT IS A PORPOISE?

A porpoise is a small whale with a rounded head, not a beaked snout like a dolphin. There are about six species of porpoise, which live in coastal waters in the Atlantic and Pacific. They feed on fish and squid.

IS A DOLPHIN A KIND OF WHALE?

A dolphin is a small whale. Most of the 37 or so species of dolphin live in the sea, but there are five that live in rivers. The biggest dolphin is usually known as the killer whale, or orca, and grows up to 31 feet long. Dolphins have a streamlined shape and a beaked snout containing lots of sharp teeth. They are fast swimmers and they catch sea creatures such as fish and squid to eat. A form of ultrasound helps dolphins find their prey. A dolphin gives off a series of high-frequency clicking sounds that bounce off anything in their path. The echoes tell the dolphin about the size and direction of the prey.

Blue whales once lived in all oceans. Now most are found in Antarctic waters.

DO WHALES GIVE BIRTH IN THE WATER?

Yes, they do. The baby whale comes out of the mother's body tail first so that it does not drown during birth. As soon as the head emerges, the mother and the other females attending the birth help the baby whale swim to the surface to take its first breath.

ARE FLATFISHES BORN FLAT?

No, they are not. Young flatfishes have normal bodies with an eye on each side. As they grow, the body flattens and one eye moves, so that both are on the upper surface. The fish lies on the seabed with its eyed side uppermost so it can see.

The shark's teeth may be up to 3 inches long.

WHICH IS THE FIERCEST FRESHWATER FISH?

The piranha, which lives in rivers in tropical Central and South America, is the fiercest of all freshwater fish. Each fish is only about 12 inches long, but a shoal of hundreds attacking together can kill and eat a much larger animal in seconds. The piranha's weapons are its extremely sharp triangular-shaped teeth, which it uses to chop flesh from its victim. But not all piranhas are dangerous killers. Some species feed only on plants.

GREAT WHITE SHARK

ARE ALL SHARKS KILLERS?

No, two of the largest sharks, the whale shark and the basking shark, eat only tiny shrimp-like creatures. They filter these from the water through special sieve-like structures in the mouth.

This fish puffs up its body when in danger.

PUFFER FISH

ARE THERE ANY POISONOUS FISH?

Yes, there are—and the puffer fish is one of the most poisonous of all. It has a powerful poison in some of its internal organs, such as the heart and liver, which can kill a human. Despite this, puffer fish is a delicacy in Japan, where chefs are specially trained to remove the poisonous parts and prepare the fish. A puffer fish also has another way of defending itself. It can puff its body up with water and air until it is at least twice its normal size. This makes it very hard for any predator to swallow. Some puffer fish are covered with spines that stick up when the body is inflated.

ARE ELECTRIC EELS REALLY ELECTRIC?

Yes, they are. The electric eel's body contains special muscles that can release electrical charges into the water. These are powerful enough to stun and kill its prey.

WHY DOES A FLYING FISH "FLY?"

A flying fish usually lifts itself above the water to escape from danger. It has extra large fins, which act as its "wings." After building up speed in the water, the fish lifts its fins and glides above the surface for a short distance.

HOW FAST DO FISH SWIM?

The sailfish is one of the fastest swimming fish. It has been timed moving at speeds of more than 62 mph. Marlins and tunas are also fast swimmers. All these fish have sleek streamlined bodies.

HOW BIG IS A GREAT WHITE SHARK?

Great white sharks are mostly about 23 feet long, but some can grow up to 40 feet. They live in warm seas all over the world. Great white sharks are fierce hunters and attack large fish and other creatures such as sea lions and porpoises. Their main weapons are their large, jagged-edged teeth, which they use to kill prey and to tear it apart. Behind these teeth are rows of new ones, ready to replace teeth at the front that get damaged or broken.

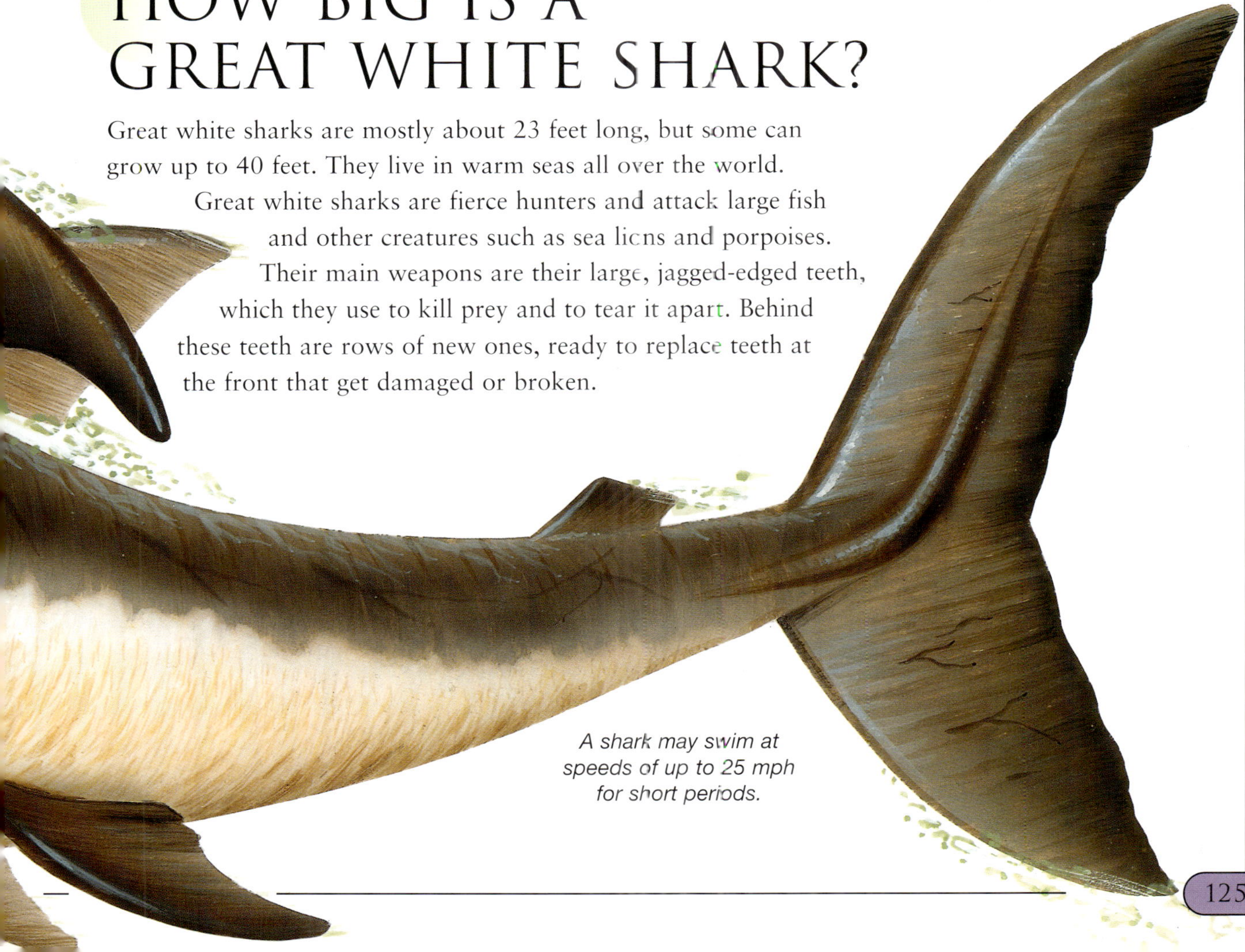

A shark may swim at speeds of up to 25 mph for short periods.

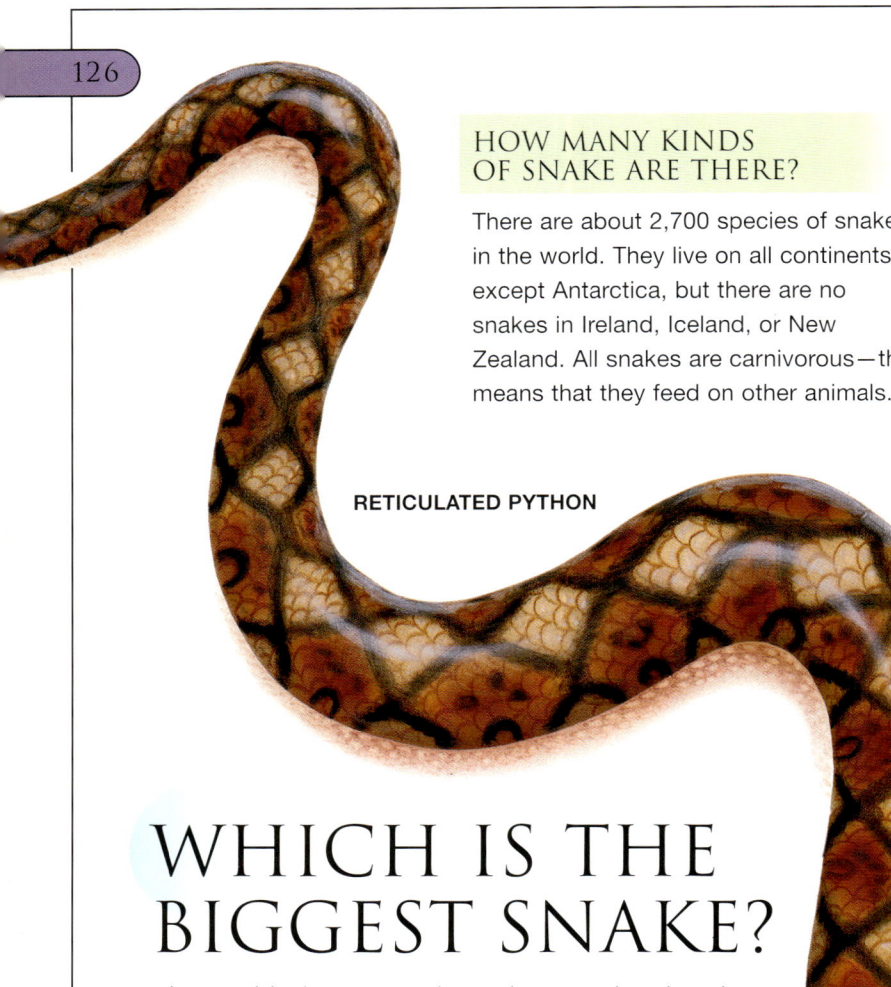

RETICULATED PYTHON

HOW MANY KINDS OF SNAKE ARE THERE?

There are about 2,700 species of snake in the world. They live on all continents except Antarctica, but there are no snakes in Ireland, Iceland, or New Zealand. All snakes are carnivorous—that means that they feed on other animals.

ARE ALL SNAKES POISONOUS?

Only about a third of all snakes are poisonous and fewer still have poison strong enough to harm humans. Non-poisonous snakes either crush their prey to death or simply swallow it whole.

WHY DOES A RATTLESNAKE RATTLE?

Rattlesnakes make their rattling noise to warn their enemies to stay well away. The rattle is made by a number of hard rings of skin at the end of the tail that make a noise when shaken. Each ring was once the tip of the tail. A new one is added every time the snake grows and sheds its skin.

WHICH IS THE BIGGEST SNAKE?

The world's longest snake is the reticulated python, which lives in parts of Southeast Asia. It grows to an amazing 33 feet. The anaconda, which lives in South American rainforests, is heavier than the python but not quite as long. Pythons and anacondas are not poisonous snakes. They kill with their teeth or by crushing prey to death. A python lies in wait for its prey, then creeps up and wraps the victim in the powerful coils of its body until it is suffocated.

The python can coil its strong body around its prey and crush it to death.

WHICH IS THE MOST DANGEROUS SNAKE?

The saw-scaled carpet viper is probably the world's most dangerous snake. It is extremely aggressive and its poison can kill humans. Saw-scaled carpet vipers live in Africa and Asia.

ARE THERE ANY SNAKES IN THE SEA?

Yes, there are about 47 different species of snake that spend their whole lives in the sea. Most are completely helpless on land. They eat fish and other sea creatures, such as shrimp, and all are extremely poisonous. One, the beaked sea snake, has the deadliest poison of any snake.

WHY DO SNAKES SHED THEIR SKIN?

Snakes shed their skin, or molt, to allow for growth and because their skin gets worn and damaged. In its first year, when it is growing quickly, a young snake may shed its skin seven times or more. After this, it may only molt once a year or less.

HOW FAST DO SNAKES MOVE?

The fastest-moving snake on land is thought to be the black mamba, which lives in Africa. It can wriggle along at up to 12 mph.

WHY DOES A CHAMELEON CHANGE COLOR?

Changing color helps the chameleon get near to its prey without being seen and allows it to hide from its own enemies. The color change is controlled by the chameleon's nervous system. Nerves cause areas of color in the skin to be spread out or to become concentrated in tiny dots. Chameleons are also said to go darker in color when angry and lighter when afraid.

CHAMELEON

ARE THERE ANY POISONOUS LIZARDS?

There are only two poisonous lizards in the world—the gila monster and the Mexican beaded lizard, both of which live in western North America. The poison is made in glands in the lower jaw. When the lizard seizes a prey and starts to chew, poison flows into the wound. Overpowered by the poison, the victim soon stops struggling.

HOW MANY KINDS OF LIZARD ARE THERE?

There are about 3,000 different species of lizard. These belong to different groups, or families, such as the geckos, iguanas, skinks, and chameleons. There are lizards on all continents, except Antarctica, but most live in warm parts of the world.

WHERE DO CHAMELEONS LIVE?

There are about 85 different sorts of chameleon and most of these live in Africa and Madagascar. There are a few Asian species and one kind of chameleon lives in parts of southern Europe.

WHICH IS THE LARGEST LIZARD?

The komodo dragon, which lives on some Southeast Asian islands. It grows up to 10 feet long and hunts animals such as wild pigs and small deer.

The python's jaws open extremely wide so it can swallow prey larger than itself.

HARPY EAGLE

WHICH IS THE BIGGEST EAGLE?

The biggest eagle in the world is the harpy eagle, which lives in rainforests in South America. It is up to 43 inches long and has huge feet and sharp talons, which it uses to kill its prey. Unlike other eagles, the harpy does not soar high in the air looking for food. It hunts creatures such as monkeys and sloths in the trees, chasing its victims from branch to branch at high speed. Almost as big is the rare Philippine monkey-eating eagle, which lives in rainforests in the Philippines.

The harpy eagle has shorter wings than other eagles so that it can fly among the branches of rainforest trees.

DO EAGLES BUILD NESTS?

Yes, and the nest made by the bald eagle is the biggest made by any bird. Some bald eagle nests are up to 18 feet deep. They are used again and again and the eagles add more nest material each year.

The peregrine falcon is a fast, strong flier and hunts from several hundred feet in the air.

PEREGRINE FALCON

WHICH IS THE FASTEST FLYING BIRD?

As it dives to catch other birds in the air, the peregrine falcon may move at more than 100 mph, faster than any other bird. The falcon circles above its victim before making its fast dive and killing the prey with a blow from its powerful talons.

DO EAGLES REALLY CATCH SNAKES?

Yes, serpent eagles feed mostly on snakes and lizards. The rough surface of the serpent eagle's toes helps it hold on to slippery snakes.

HOW DO EAGLES KILL THEIR PREY?

An eagle kills with the four long curved claws on each of its feet. It drops down on to the victim, seizes it in its long talons and crushes it to death. The eagle then tears the flesh apart with its strong hooked beak. The hook of a golden eagle's beak is as much as 4 inches long.

WHAT DOES AN OSPREY EAT?

The osprey feeds mostly on fish. When it sees something near the surface, it dives down toward the water and seizes the fish in its feet. The soles of its feet are covered with small spines to help it hold on to the slippery fish.

WHICH IS THE BIGGEST BIRD OF PREY?

The Andean condor is the biggest bird of prey in the world. It measures up to 43 inches long and weighs up to 25 lb. Its wingspan is over 10 feet.

HOW CAN OWLS HUNT AT NIGHT?

Owls have excellent sight, even in low light, and extremely sharp hearing. Even in complete darkness they can pinpoint where a sound is coming from and swoop. Owls also have special soft-edged wing feathers which make very little noise as they beat their wings. This allows them to approach prey with scarcely a sound.

HOW MANY KINDS OF OWL ARE THERE?

There are about 142 different species of owl in two different families. The barn owl family contains about 12 species and the true owl family about 130 species. Owls live in most parts of the world, except a few islands. They usually hunt at night, catching small mammals, birds, frogs, lizards, insects, and even fish.

DO VULTURES HUNT AND KILL PREY?

Vultures do not usually kill their prey. They are scavengers, feeding on animals that are already dead or have been killed by hunters such as lions. They have strong claws and beaks and the bald head allows them to plunge into carcasses without dirtying their feathers. The bearded vulture, or lammergeier, often picks up bones, which it drops on to rocks to smash them open. It can then feed on the marrow inside.

The bearded vulture gets its name from the clump of black bristles that hangs under its beak.

BEARDED VULTURES GATHERING AT A CARCASS

SECTION EIGHT

HOW DOES IT WORK?

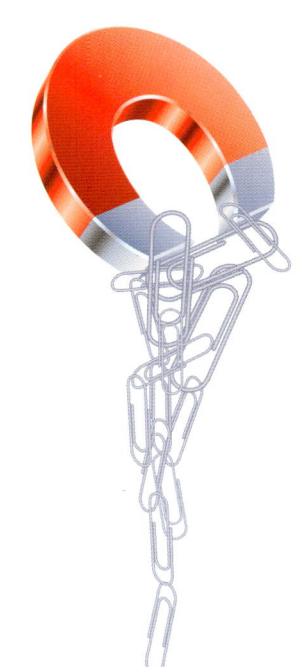

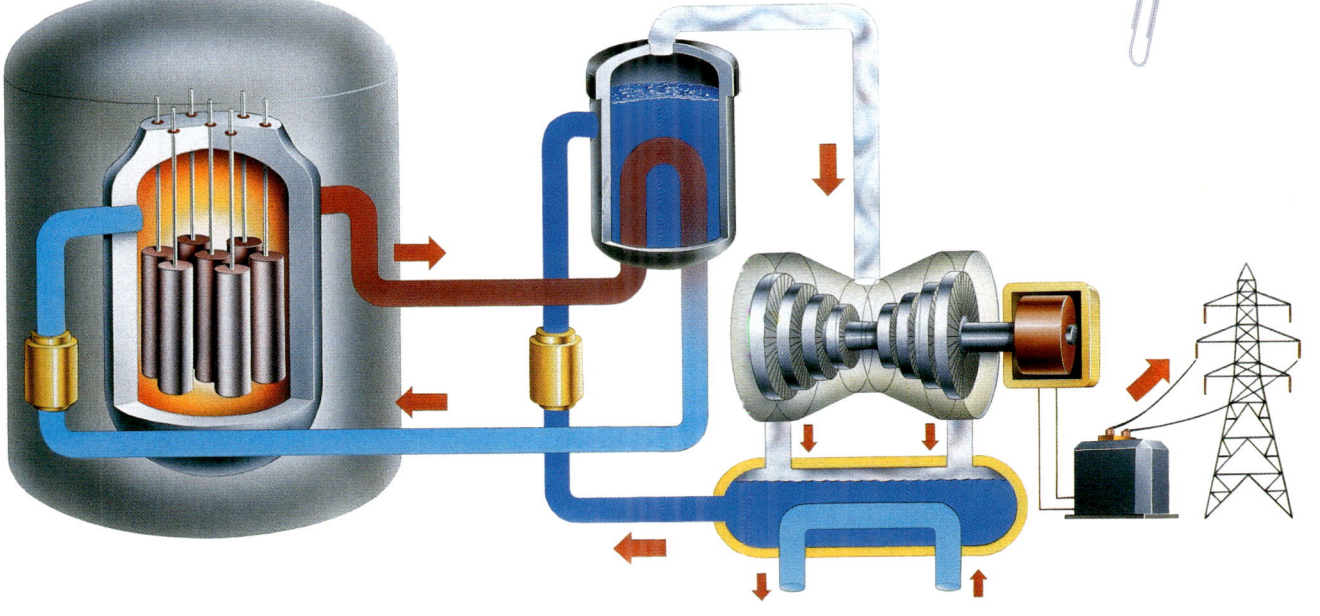

WHAT ARE SOLIDS?

Substances can be either solid, liquid, or gas—the three 'states of matter." Substances move from one state to another when they are heated or cooled—boosting or reducing the energy of the particles they are made of. In solids, particles are locked together, so solids have a definite shape and volume. In liquids, particles move around a bit, so liquids can flow into any shape—but stay the same volume. In gases, particles zoom about all over the place, so gases spread out to fill containers of any size or shape. When a substance is normally a liquid but turns into a gas, this is called a vapor.

WHAT IS A PLASMA?

A plasma is the rare fourth state of matter. It occurs only when a gas becomes so hot its particles break up. This happens inside the Sun and in gas neon tubes.

WHEN DO THINGS MELT?

Things melt from solid to liquid on reaching a temperature called the melting point. Each substance has its own melting point. Water's is 32°F; lead's is 621.5°F.

WHEN DO THINGS FREEZE?

Things freeze from liquid to solid when they reach the freezing point, which is the same as melting point. Most substances get smaller when they freeze as the particles pack closer together. Water gets bigger as it turns to ice, which is why frozen pipes burst in winter.

WHEN DO THINGS BOIL?

Things boil from liquid to gas when they reach boiling point, which is the maximum temperature a liquid can reach. For water this is 212°F. An increase in pressure increases boiling point, which is why pressure cookers allow things to cook at higher temperatures.

WATER AS SOLID, LIQUID, AND GAS

Solids do not keep their shape completely. The ice in glaciers can flow very slowly.

THUNDERCLOUDS

Large thunderclouds are made from water droplets and ice crystals.

HOW DOES PRESSURE CHANGE?

If you squeeze a gas into half the space, the pressure doubles (as long as the temperature stays the same). This is Boyle's law. If you warm a gas up, the pressure rises in proportion (as long as you keep it the same volume). This is the Pressure law.

WHAT HAPPENS IN EVAPORATION AND CONDENSATION?

Evaporation happens when a liquid is warmed up and changes to a vapor. Particles at the liquid's surface vibrate so fast they escape altogether. Condensation happens when a vapor is cooled down and becomes liquid. Evaporation and condensation take place not only at boiling point, but also at much cooler temperatures.

WHAT IS PRESSURE?

Pressure is the amount of force pressing on something. Air pressure is the force with which air presses. The force comes from the bombardment of the moving air particles. The more particles there are, and the faster they are moving, the greater the pressure.

Clouds form when rising air gets so cold that the water vapor it contains condenses into water droplets.

WHAT IS AN ELEMENT?

It is a substance that cannot be split up into other substances. Water is not an element because it can be split into the gases oxygen and hydrogen. Oxygen and hydrogen are elements because they cannot be split. Every element has its own atomic number. This is the number of protons in its nucleus, which is balanced by the same number of electrons.

WHAT IS THE LIGHTEST ELEMENT?

The lightest element is hydrogen. It has just one proton in its nucleus and has an atomic mass of just one.

WHO DISCOVERED RADIUM?

The Polish-French physicist Marie Curie (1867–1934), born Marya Sklodowska, is the only woman to have won two Nobel prizes—one in 1903 for her part in the discovery of radioactivity, and one in 1911 for her discovery of the elements polonium and radium.

FLUORINE

SILVER

WHAT IS A METAL?

Most people can recognize a metal. It is hard, dense, and shiny, and goes "ping" when you strike it with something else made of metal. It also conducts both electricity and heat well. Chemists define a metal as an electropositive element, which basically means that metals easily lose negatively charged electrons. It is these lost, "free" electrons that make metals such excellent conductors of electricity.

HOW MANY ELEMENTS ARE THERE?

New elements are discovered every so often, but the total number identified so far is 112.

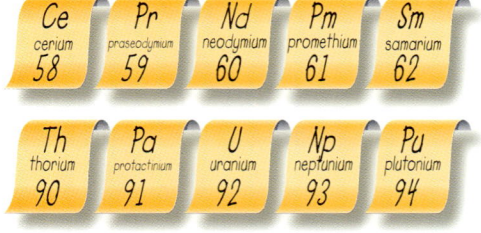

WHAT IS THE HEAVIEST ELEMENT?

The heaviest is hahnium. It has 105 protons and 157 neutrons in its nucleus. The atomic mass of hahnium is 262.

GOLD

WHY ARE SOME ELEMENTS REACTIVE?

Elements are reactive if they readily gain or lose electrons. Elements on the left of the periodic table, called metals, lose electrons very easily—the further left they are, the more reactive they are. So Group I metals (called the alkali metals) including sodium, potassium, and francium are very reactive.

COPPER

WHAT IS THE PERIODIC TABLE?

All the elements can be ordered according to their properties, forming a chart called the periodic table. Columns are called groups, rows are called periods. Elements in the same group have the same number of electrons in the outer shell of their atoms and similar properties.

URANIUM

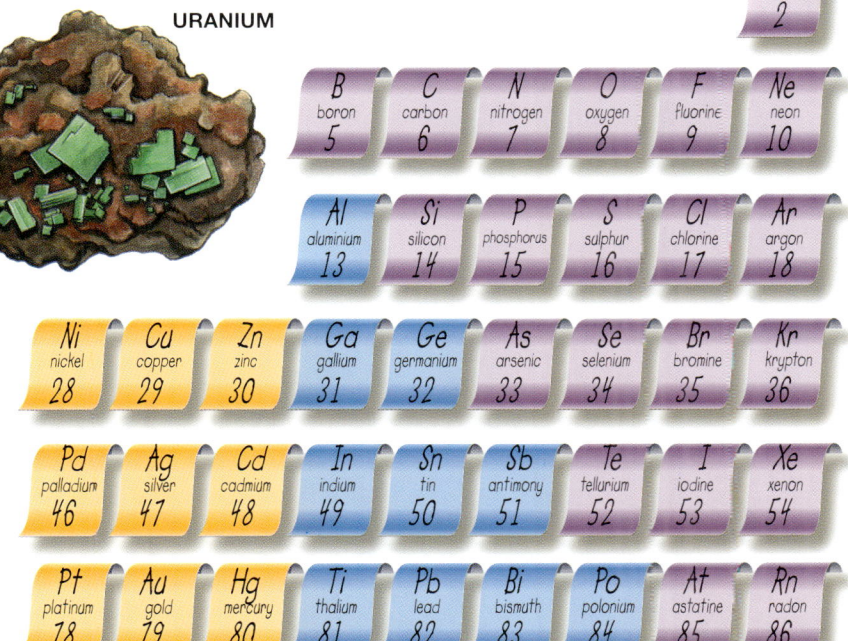

He
helium
2

| B boron 5 | C carbon 6 | N nitrogen 7 | O oxygen 8 | F fluorine 9 | Ne neon 10 |
| Al aluminium 13 | Si silicon 14 | P phosphorus 15 | S sulphur 16 | Cl chlorine 17 | Ar argon 18 |

Ni nickel 28	Cu copper 29	Zn zinc 30	Ga gallium 31	Ge germanium 32	As arsenic 33	Se selenium 34	Br bromine 35	Kr krypton 36
Pd palladium 46	Ag silver 47	Cd cadmium 48	In indium 49	Sn tin 50	Sb antimony 51	Te tellurium 52	I iodine 53	Xe xenon 54
Pt platinum 78	Au gold 79	Hg mercury 80	Ti thalium 81	Pb lead 82	Bi bismuth 83	Po polonium 84	At astatine 85	Rn radon 86

| Eu europium 63 | Gd gadolinium 64 | Tb terbium 65 | Dy dysprosium 66 | Ho holmium 67 | Er erbium 68 | Tm thalium 69 | Yb ytterbium 70 | Lu lutetium 71 |
| Am americium 95 | Cm curium 96 | Bk berkelium 97 | Cf californium 98 | Es einsteinium 99 | Fm fermium 100 | Md mendelevium 101 | No nobelium 102 | Lr lawrencium 103 |

The actinides are a group of 15 elements at the bottom of the periodic table that take their name from actinium. They include radium and plutonium and are all very radioactive.

BISMUTH

WHAT ARE NOBLE GASES?

Group 0 is the furthest right-hand column of the periodic table. This group is called the noble gases, because they have full-up outer electron shells and so nobly stay aloof from any reaction with "base" metals or any other substance. They are sometimes called inert gases.

WHY IS CARBON SO SPECIAL?

Carbon is the most friendly element in the Universe. With four electrons in the outer shell of its atom (and so four gaps), carbon atoms link very readily with other atoms.

SULPHUR

WHAT IS ATOMIC MASS?

Atomic mass is the "weight" of one whole atom of a substance—which is of course very tiny! It includes all the particles in the atom—protons, neutrons, and electrons.

WHAT IS AN ATOM?

Atoms are what every substance is made of. Atoms are the smallest recognizable bit of any substance. They are so small that they are visible only under extremely high-powered microscopes—you could fit two billion atoms on the full stop at the end of this sentence. Yet atoms are largely composed of empty space—empty space dotted with even tinier clouds of energy called sub-atomic particles.

HOW BIG ARE ATOMS?

Atoms are about a ten millionth of a millimetre across and weigh 100 trillionths of a trillionth of a gram. The smallest atom is hydrogen; the biggest is meitnerium. (Since they are so small, atoms are measured in terms of "moles," which is a quantity of the substance containing the same number of atoms as 12 grams of a form of carbon called Carbon 12.)

HOW MANY KINDS OF PARTICLE ARE THERE?

Since the 1920s, scientists have discovered that there are at least 200 kinds of sub-atomic particle besides electrons, protons, and neutrons. Most of these are created in special conditions and exist only for a fraction of a second at a time.

WHAT IS A MOLECULE?

Quite often, atoms cannot exist by themselves, and must always join up with others—either of the same kind, or with other kinds to form chemical compounds. A molecule is the smallest particle of a substance that can exist on its own.

WHAT IS THE SMALLEST PARTICLE OF ALL?

No one is sure. Atoms are made of protons, neutrons, and electrons. In turn, these could be made of even tinier particles—quarks and leptons. But one day, we might discover even smaller particles...

WHAT ARE ELECTRONS?

Electrons are the very tiny electrically charged particles that whizz round inside an atom. They were discovered by the English physicist J.J. Thomson (1856–1940) in 1879 during some experiments with cathode ray tubes. (Computer and TV screens are cathode ray tubes, and cathode rays are actually streams of electrons.)

INSIDE A PROTON

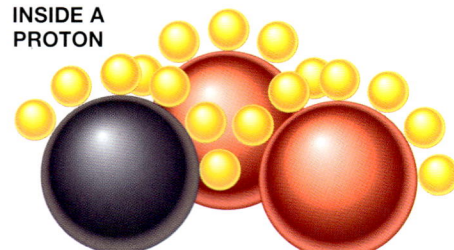

Protons may be made of even smaller particles— quarks joined by gluons.

WHAT HOLDS ATOMS TOGETHER?

Electrons are held to the nucleus by electrical attraction— because they have an opposite electrical charge to the protons in the nucleus. The particles of the nucleus are held together by a force called the strong nuclear force.

AN ATOM

WHAT ARE ELECTRON SHELLS?

Electrons behave as if they are stacked around the nucleus at different levels, like the layers of an onion. These levels are called shells, and there is room for only a particular number of electrons in each shell. The number of electrons in the outer shell determines how the atom will react with other atoms. An atom with a full outer shell, like the gas argon, is unresponsive. An atom with room for one or more extra electrons in its outer shell, like oxygen, is very reactive.

Around the nucleus whirls a cloud of tiny negatively charged electrons.

At the center of an atom is the nucleus, made from protons and neutrons.

WHAT IS AN ION?

An ion is an atom that has either lost one or a few electrons, making it positively charged (cation) or gained a few, making it negatively charged (anion). Ions usually form when substances dissolve in a liquid.

WHAT IS THE NUCLEUS?

Most of an atom is empty space, but right at its center is a very tiny area that is densely packed with particles much bigger than electrons. This is the nucleus, and it usually contains two kinds of nuclear particle—neutrons with no electrical charge, and protons with a positive electrical charge (opposite to the negative charge of electrons).

WHY IS NUCLEAR POWER AWESOME?

The energy that binds together an atomic nucleus is enormous, even though the nucleus itself is so small. In fact, as Einstein showed in 1905 with his theory of Special Relativity, the particles of the nucleus can also be regarded as pure energy. This enables nuclear power stations to generate huge amounts of power with just a few tons of nuclear fuel. It also gives nuclear bombs a massive and terrifying destructive power.

WHAT EXACTLY IS RADIOACTIVITY?

The atoms of an element may come in several different forms or isotopes. Each form has a different number of neutrons in the nucleus, indicated in the name, as in carbon-12 and carbon-14. The nuclei of some of these isotopes—the ones scientists call radioisotopes—are unstable, and they decay (break up), releasing radiation, consisting of streams of particles called alpha, beta, and gamma rays. This is what radioactivity is.

A containment building houses the reactor vessel, keeping in heat, radioactivity, and other energy.

WHAT DOES RADIATION DO TO YOU?

It causes radiation sickness. With a very high dose, the victim dies in a few hours from nerve damage. With a less high dose, the victim dies after a week or so from damage to the gut or a complete collapse of the body's resistance to disease. Lower doses of radiation can cause cancer (including leukemia) and defects in newborn babies.

NUCLEAR FISSION

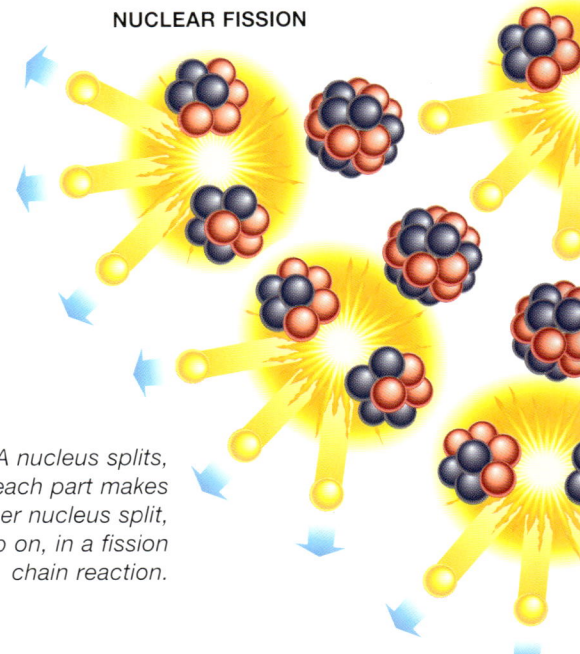

A nucleus splits, and each part makes another nucleus split, and so on, in a fission chain reaction.

Warmth from the nuclear reaction superheats water under very high pressure in the primary loop.

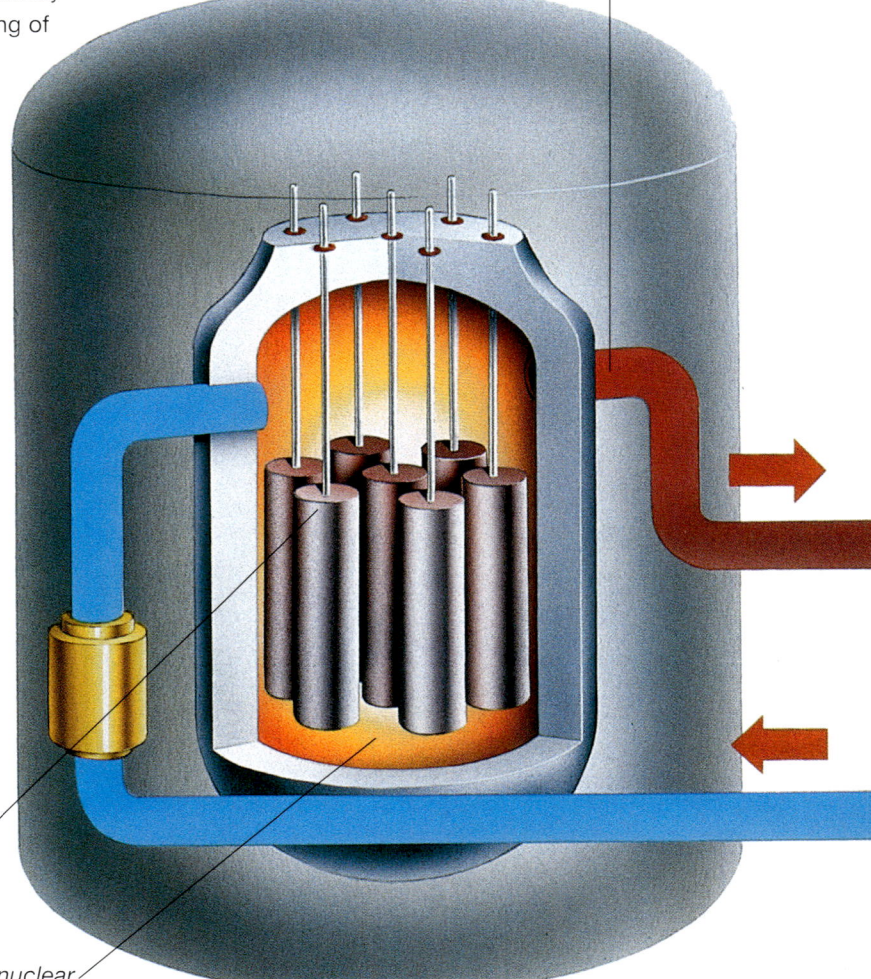

The nuclear reactions take place in fuel rods in the reactor core.

In the reactor vessel, nuclear fission releases tremendous amounts of heat energy.

A NUCLEAR POWER STATION

WHAT IS NUCLEAR FUSION?

Nuclear energy is released by fusing or joining together small atoms like those of deuterium (a form of hydrogen). Nuclear fusion is the reaction that keeps stars glowing and provides energy for thermonuclear warheads. Scientists hope to find a way of harnessing nuclear fusion for power generation.

WHAT IS NUCLEAR FISSION?

Nuclear fission releases nuclear energy by splitting big atomic nuclei—usually those of uranium. Neutrons are fired at the nuclei. As the neutrons smash into the nuclei they split off more neutrons, which bombard other nuclei, setting off a chain reaction.

The superheated water in the primary loop boils water in the secondary loop into high-pressure steam.

WHO INVENTED THE ATOMIC BOMB?

The first atomic bombs were developed in the USA toward the end of the Second World War by a brilliant team of scientists under the leadership of Robert Oppenheimer (1904–1967). His colleagues included Leo Szilard (1898–1964) and Otto Frisch (1904–1979). Together they created the first two A-bombs, which were dropped on Hiroshima and Nagasaki in Japan in 1945 with devastating effect.

WHAT IS AN ATOMIC BOMB?

An atomic bomb or A-bomb is one of the two main kinds of nuclear weapon. An A-bomb relies on the explosive nuclear fission of uranium-235 or plutonium-239. Hydrogen bombs, also called H-bombs or thermonuclear weapons, rely on the fusion of hydrogen atoms to create explosions a thousand times more powerful.

HOW DO NUCLEAR POWER STATIONS WORK?

Inside the reactor there are fuel rods made from pellets of uranium dioxide, separated by spacers. When the station goes "on-line," a nuclear fission chain reaction is set up in the fuel rods. This is slowed down by control rods, which absorb the neutrons so that heat is produced steadily to drive the steam turbines that generate electricity.

The steam passes through the turbines.

High-pressure steam spins the turbine blades.

The turbine blades turn the electricity generator.

Pumps keep the water moving round the circuits.

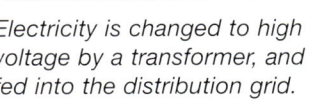

Electricity is changed to high voltage by a transformer, and fed into the distribution grid.

The cooler water flows back to the reactor for reheating.

The steam condenses into liquid water.

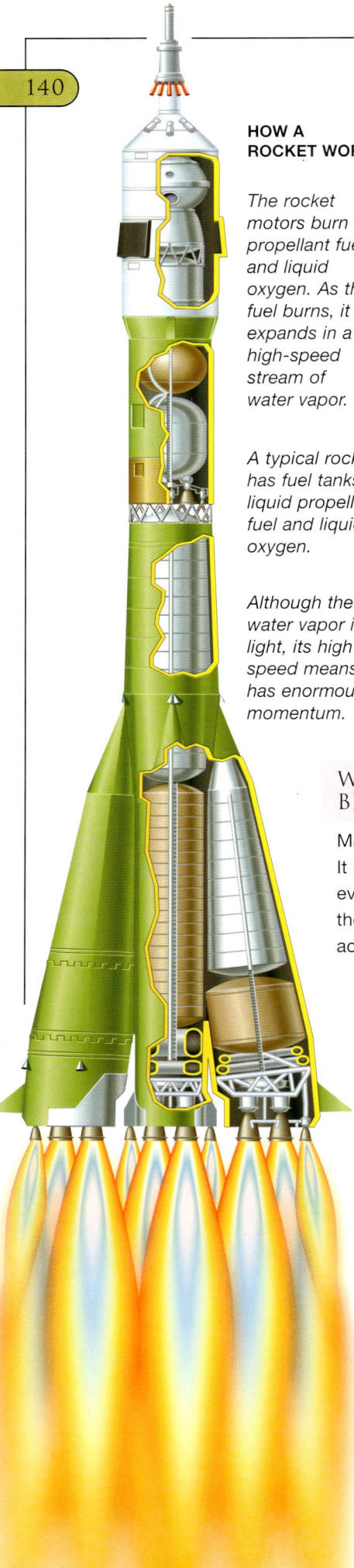

HOW A ROCKET WORKS

The rocket motors burn the propellant fuel and liquid oxygen. As the fuel burns, it expands in a high-speed stream of water vapor.

A typical rocket has fuel tanks of liquid propellant fuel and liquid oxygen.

Although the water vapor is light, its high speed means it has enormous momentum.

In accordance with Newton's Law of Motion, the momentum of the gas gives the rocket an equal momentum in the opposite direction, thrusting it upward.

WHAT IS A FORCE?

A force is what makes something move—by pushing it or pulling it in a particular direction. It may be an invisible force, like gravity, or a visible force like a kick, but it always causes something to either accelerate or decelerate or change shape. Forces always work in pairs—whenever a force pushes, it must push against something else equally—which is why guns kick back violently when fired.

WHAT IS POWER?

Power is the rate at which work is done—a high-powered engine is an engine that can move a great deal of weight very quickly. Power is also the rate at which energy is transferred—a large amount of electric power might be needed to heat a large quantity of water.

WHAT IS FRICTION?

Friction is the force between two things rubbing together, which may be brake pads on a bicycle wheel or air molecules against an airplane. Friction tends to slow things down, making them hot as their momentum is converted into heat.

WHAT'S THE DIFFERENCE BETWEEN MASS AND WEIGHT?

Mass is the amount of matter in an object. It is the same wherever you measure it, even on the Moon. Weight is a measure of the force of gravity on an object. It varies according to where you measure it.

WHAT IS GRAVITY?

Gravity is the invisible force of attraction between every bit of matter in the Universe. Its strength depends on the mass of the objects involved and their distance apart.

WHAT DID A GREAT SCIENTIST LEARN FROM AN APPLE?

The mathematician and physicist Sir Isaac Newton is said to have developed his ideas about gravity while sitting one day under an apple tree. As he watched an apple fall to the ground, it occurred to him in a flash that the apple was not merely falling but was being pulled toward the ground by an invisible force. This is the force he called gravity.

WHAT DID GALILEO DO ON THE TOWER OF PISA?

The Italian scientist and astronomer Galileo Galilei (1564–1642) is said to have dropped metal balls of different weights from the Leaning Tower of Pisa to show that they all fall at the same speed.

HOW IS FORCE MEASURED?

Force is measured in newtons, in honor of Sir Isaac Newton. A newton is the force needed to accelerate 1 kilogram by 1 meter per second every second.

WHY DO SATELLITES GO ROUND THE EARTH?

Satellites are whizzing through space at exactly the right height for their speed. The Earth's gravity tries to pull them down to Earth, but they are traveling so fast that they go on zooming round the Earth just as fast as the Earth pulls them in.

HOW DOES GRAVITY HOLD YOU DOWN?

The mutual gravitational attraction between the mass of your body and the mass of the Earth pulls them together. If you jump off a wall, the Earth pulls you toward the ground. You also pull the Earth toward you, but because you are tiny while the Earth is huge, you move a lot and the Earth barely moves at all.

WHY CAN YOU JUMP HIGHER ON THE MOON?

The Moon is much smaller than the Earth, so its gravity is much weaker. Astronauts weigh six times less on the Moon than they do on Earth—and can jump much higher!

DOES GRAVITY VARY?

An object's gravitational pull varies with its mass and its distance. In fact, gravity diminishes precisely in proportion to its distance away, squared. You can work out the force of gravity between two objects by multiplying their masses and dividing by the square of the distance between them. This sum works all over the Universe with pinpoint accuracy.

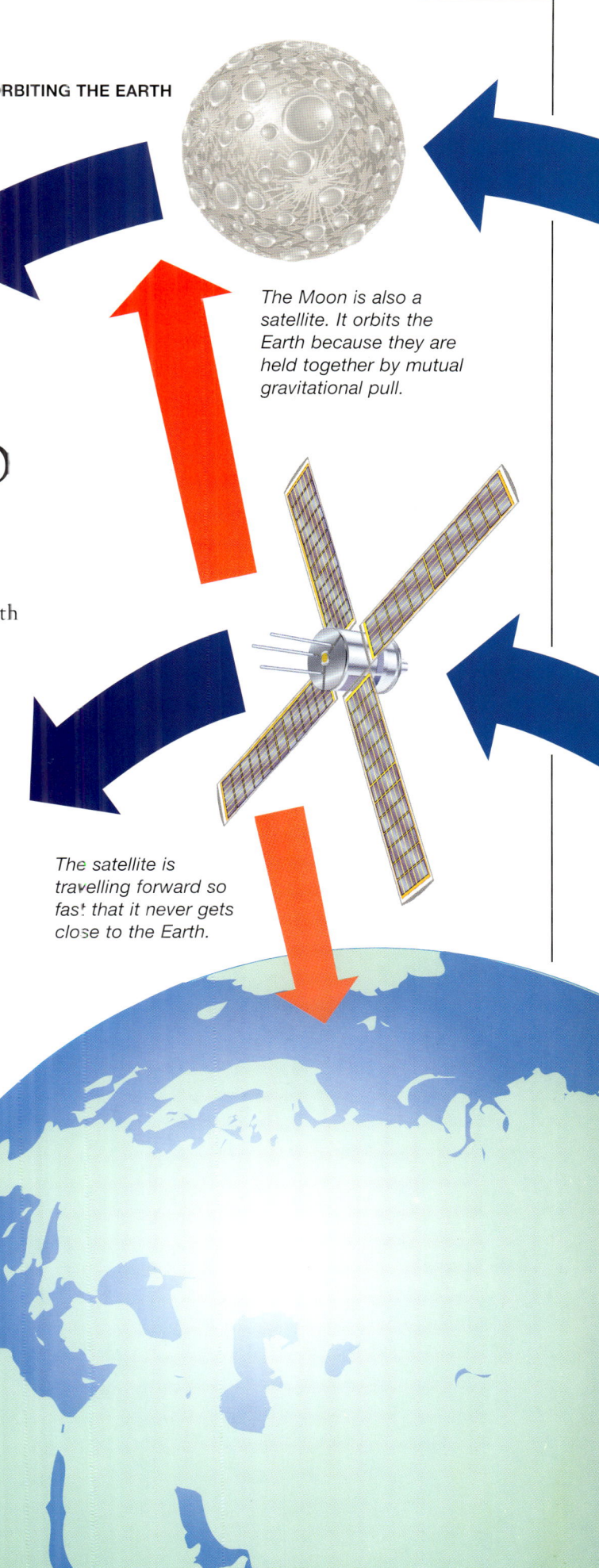

ORBITING THE EARTH

The Moon is also a satellite. It orbits the Earth because they are held together by mutual gravitational pull.

The satellite is travelling forward so fast that it never gets close to the Earth.

Gravity is tugging the satellite downward all the time.

All the different colors of light have different wavelengths. The longest waves we can see are red.

HOW DO TV SIGNALS TRAVEL?

TV signals travel in one of three ways. Terrestrial broadcasts are beamed out from transmitters as radio waves to be picked up by TV aerials. Satellite broadcasts are sent up to satellites as microwaves, then picked up by satellite dishes. Cable broadcasts travel as electrical or light signals along underground cables, straight to the TV set.

Rainbows are formed by the reflection of the Sun off billions of drops of moisture in the air.

WHAT ARE THE COLORS OF THE RAINBOW?

The colors of the rainbow are all the colors contained in white light. When white light hits raindrops in the air, it is split up into a rainbow of colors, because each color of light is refracted by the rainbow to a different extent. The colors of the rainbow appear in this order: red, orange, yellow, green, blue, indigo, violet.

WHY CAN'T YOU SEE ULTRAVIOLET?

Ultraviolet light is light with wavelengths too short for the human eye to register.

WHAT IS THE ELECTROMAGNETIC SPECTRUM?

Light is just a small part of the wide range of radiation emitted by atoms—the only part we can see. This range of radiation is called the electromagnetic spectrum and ranges from long waves—such as radio waves and microwaves—to short waves —such as X-rays and gamma rays.

HOW DO X-RAYS SEE THROUGH YOU?

X-rays are stopped only by the bones and especially dense bits of the body. They pass through the soft bits to hit a photographic plate on the far side of the body, where they leave a silhouette of the skeleton.

HOW DO CT SCANS WORK?

CT (computed tomography) scans run X-ray beams right round the body, and pick up how much is absorbed with special sensors. A computer analyzes the data to create a complete "slice" through the body.

ELECTROMAGNETIC SPECTRUM

The shortest waves of light we can see are violet.

WHAT IS INFRARED?

Infrared is light with wavelengths too long for the human eye to register. But you can often feel infrared light as warmth.

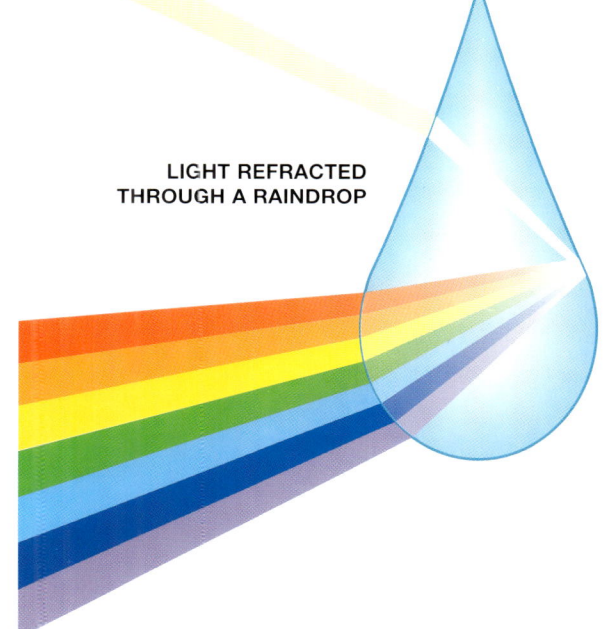

LIGHT REFRACTED THROUGH A RAINDROP

HOW DOES A PRISM SPLIT COLORS?

Prisms split white light into separate colors by refracting (bending) it. The longer the wavelength of the light, the more it is refracted. So long wavelength colors emerge from the prism at a different point from short wavelength colors.

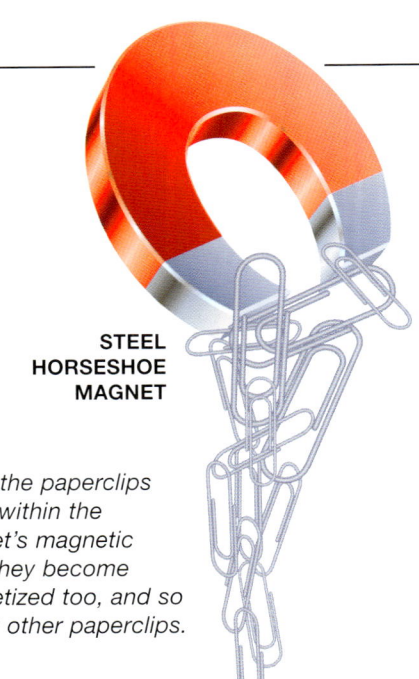

STEEL HORSESHOE MAGNET

When the paperclips come within the magnet's magnetic field, they become magnetized too, and so attract other paperclips.

WHAT IS RESONANCE?

If allowed to vibrate freely, every object always tends to vibrate at the same rate. This is its natural frequency. You can make things vibrate faster or slower than this by jogging them at particular intervals. But if you can jog it at just the same rate as its natural frequency, it vibrates in sympathy and the vibrations become much stronger. This is resonance.

HOW DOES SOUND TRAVEL?

Every sound is created by vibration, be it an elastic band twanging or a loudspeaker cone shaking to and fro. But you can't hear any sounds in a vacuum. This is because the sound reaches your ears as a vibration— and there must be something to vibrate. Normally, this is the air. When a sound source vibrates to and fro, it pushes the air around it to and fro. The sound travels through the air as it is pushed to and fro in a knock-on effect—that is by being alternately stretched and squeezed. This moving stretch and squeeze of air is called a sound wave.

WHAT IS A MAGNETIC FIELD?

The magnetic field is the area around the magnet in which its effects are felt. It gets gradually weaker further away from the magnet. The Earth's magnetic field extends some 50,000 miles out into space.

WHAT IS AN ECHO?

An echo is when you shout in a large empty hall or in a tunnel, and you hear the noise ringing back out at you a moment or two later. The echo is simply the sound of your voice bouncing back from the walls. You don't normally hear echoes, because they only bounce back clearly off smooth, hard surfaces—and in confined spaces. Even in a confined space, the wall must be at least 55 feet away, because you will hear an echo only if it bounces back at least 0.1 seconds after you shouted.

WHY IS THE EARTH LIKE A MAGNET?

As the Earth spins, the swirling of its iron core turns the core into a giant magnet. It is a little like the way a bicycle dynamo generates an electric current. Like smaller magnets, the Earth's magnet has two poles, a north and a south. It is because Earth is a magnet that small magnets always point in the same direction if allowed to swivel freely.

Short, high-frequency sound waves give high-pitched sounds.

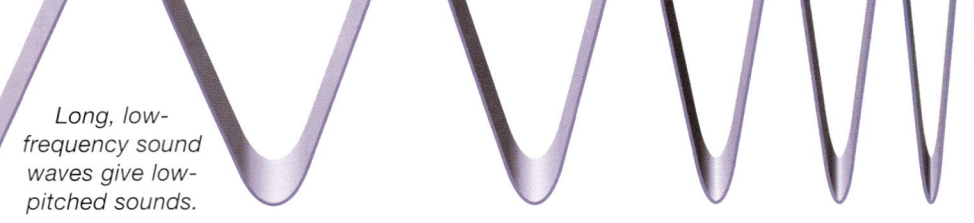

Long, low-frequency sound waves give low-pitched sounds.

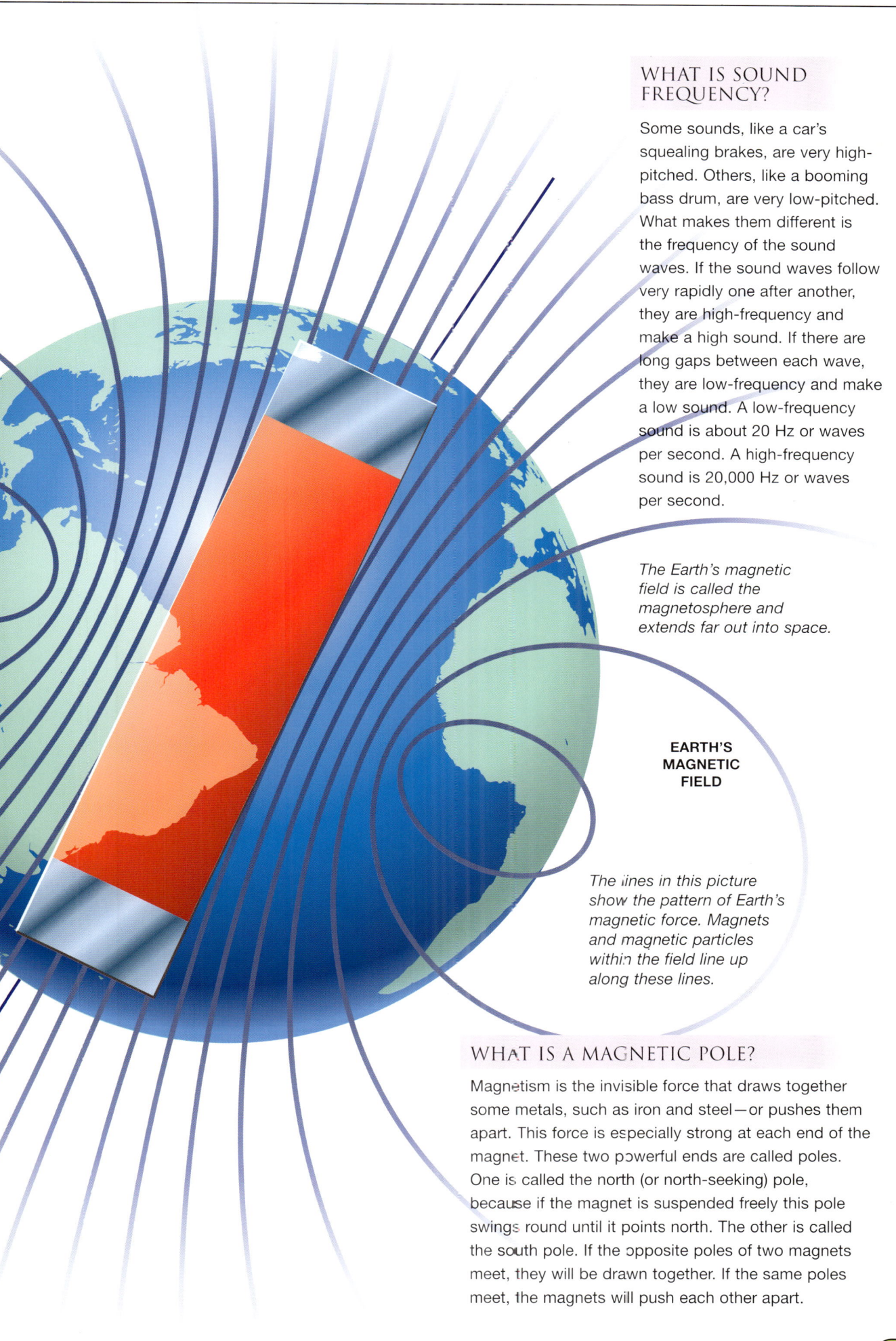

WHAT IS SOUND FREQUENCY?

Some sounds, like a car's squealing brakes, are very high-pitched. Others, like a booming bass drum, are very low-pitched. What makes them different is the frequency of the sound waves. If the sound waves follow very rapidly one after another, they are high-frequency and make a high sound. If there are long gaps between each wave, they are low-frequency and make a low sound. A low-frequency sound is about 20 Hz or waves per second. A high-frequency sound is 20,000 Hz or waves per second.

The Earth's magnetic field is called the magnetosphere and extends far out into space.

EARTH'S MAGNETIC FIELD

The lines in this picture show the pattern of Earth's magnetic force. Magnets and magnetic particles within the field line up along these lines.

WHAT IS A MAGNETIC POLE?

Magnetism is the invisible force that draws together some metals, such as iron and steel—or pushes them apart. This force is especially strong at each end of the magnet. These two powerful ends are called poles. One is called the north (or north-seeking) pole, because if the magnet is suspended freely this pole swings round until it points north. The other is called the south pole. If the opposite poles of two magnets meet, they will be drawn together. If the same poles meet, the magnets will push each other apart.

WHO DISCOVERED THE SHAPE OF DNA?

The discovery in 1953 that every molecule of DNA is shaped like a twisted rope ladder or "double helix" was one of the great scientific breakthroughs of the 20th century. Maurice Wilkins and Rosalind Franklin did the groundwork for the discovery. Francis Crick and James Watson, two young researchers at Cambridge University, UK, had the inspiration and won the Nobel Prize.

WHAT ARE AROMATICS?

Benzene is a clear liquid organic chemical found in coal tar. It can be harmful, but has many uses, for example as a cleaning fluid and in manufacturing dyes. It has distinctive hexagonal molecules made of six carbon atoms and six hydrogen atoms and called a benzene ring. It also has a distinctive aroma, which is why chemicals that have a benzene ring are called aromatics.

WHAT IS DNA?

DNA is deoxyribonucleic acid. This is the amazing long double-spiral molecule that is found inside every living cell. It is made up of long chains of sugars and phosphates linked by pairs of chemical "bases"—adenine, cytosine, guanine, and thymine. The order in which these bases recur provides in code form the instructions for all the cell's activities, and for the lifeplan of the entire organism.

The "rungs" of DNA are pairs of chemicals called bases, linked together by chemical bonds.

WHAT IS A POLYMER?

Polymers are substances made from long chains of thousands of small carbon-based molecules, called monomers, strung together. Some polymers occur naturally, such as wool and cotton, but plastics such as nylon and polythene are man-made polymers.

WHAT IS CELLULOSE?

Cellulose is a natural fiber, found in the walls of all plant cells. It is a polymer, made of long chains of sugar molecules. These long chains make it tough and stringy, which is why we can't digest it when we eat plants—it passes through our bodies largely intact.

DNA MOLECULE

WHAT IS ORGANIC CHEMISTRY?

Organic chemistry is the chemistry of carbon and its compounds. Carbon's unique atomic structure means it links atoms together in long chains, rings or other shapes to form thousands of different compounds. These include complex molecules—such as DNA—that are the basis of life, which is why carbon chemistry is called organic chemistry.

WHAT IS THE CARBON CYCLE?

Carbon circulates like this: animals breathe out carbon as carbon dioxide. Plants take in carbon dioxide from the air, convert it into carbohydrates—and when animals eat plants, they take in carbon again.

The "ropes" of the DNA molecule are alternating groups of chemicals called sugars and phosphates.

HOW IS PLASTIC MADE?

Most plastics are made from ethene, one of the products of cracked oil. When heated under pressure, the ethene molecules join in chains 30,000 or more long. These molecules get tangled like spaghetti. If the strands are held tightly together, the plastic is stiff. If the strands can slip easily over each other, the plastic is bendy, like polythene.

WHAT IS OIL?

Oils are thick liquids that won't mix with water. Mineral oils used for motor fuel are hydrocarbons— that is, complex organic chemicals made from hydrogen and carbon.

WHAT ARE CARBOHYDRATES?

Carbohydrates are chemicals made only of carbon, hydrogen and oxygen atoms—including sugars, starches and cellulose. Most animals rely on carbohydrate sugars such as glucose and sucrose for energy.

WHAT IS A CARBON CHAIN?

Carbon atoms often link together like the links of a chain to form very long thin molecules—as in the molecule of propane, which consists of three carbon atoms in a row, with hydrogen atoms attached.

This is one molecule of buckminster fullerene made from dozens of carbon atoms linked together in a ball.

WHAT ARE BUCKYBALLS?

Before 1990, carbon was known in two main forms or allotropes—diamond and graphite. In 1990, a third allotrope was created. Its molecule looks like a soccer ball or the domed stadium roofs created by American architect Buckminster Fuller. And so this allotrope is called, after him, a buckyball.

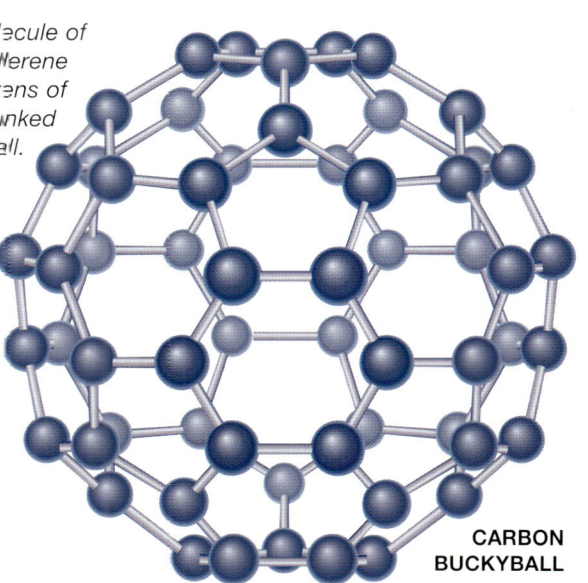

CARBON BUCKYBALL

SECTION NINE

OUT IN SPACE

HOW DID THE EARTH BEGIN?

Around four and a half billion years ago, neither the Earth nor any of the other planets existed. There was just this vast dark very hot cloud of gas and dust swirling around the newly formed Sun. Gradually, the cloud cooled and the gas began to condense into billions of droplets. Slowly these droplets were pulled together into clumps by their own gravity—and they carried on clumping until all the planets, including the Earth, were formed. But it took another half a billion years before the Earth had cooled enough to form a solid crust with an atmosphere around it.

EXACTLY HOW LONG IS A YEAR?

Every year the Earth travels once around the Sun. This epic journey measures 548,018,150 miles and takes exactly 365.24 days, which gives us our calendar year of 365 days. To make up the extra 0.24 days, we add an extra day to our calendar at the end of February in every fourth year, which is called the leap year—and then we have to knock off a leap year every four centuries.

Earth began life as hot gases and dust spiraling around the newborn Sun congealed into a ball.

WHAT'S SO SPECIAL ABOUT THE EARTH?

The Earth is the only planet with temperatures at which water can exist on the surface and is the only planet with an atmosphere containing oxygen. Water and oxygen are both needed for life.

As the Earth cooled, it gave off gases and water vapor, which formed the atmosphere.

The early Earth was a fiery ball, then the surface cooled to form a hard crust.

HOW BIG IS THE EARTH?

Satellite measurements show it is 24,870 miles around the equator and 7,927 miles across. The diameter at the Poles is slightly less, by 26.7 miles.

By 4 million years ago, the Earth's crust was covered in meteor craters and huge volcanoes.

The Earth cooled more, and the clouds of steam became water, creating vast oceans.

WHAT IS THE EARTH MADE OF?

The Earth has a core of iron and nickel, and a rocky crust made mostly of oxygen and silicon. In between is the soft hot mantle of metal silicates, sulphides, and oxides.

HOW LONG IS A DAY?

A day is the time Earth takes to turn once. The stars come back to the same place in the sky every 23 hours 56 minutes 4.09 seconds (the sidereal day). Our day (the solar day) is 24 hours because Earth is moving round the Sun, and must turn an extra 1° for the Sun to return to the same place in the sky.

HOW OLD IS THE EARTH?

The Earth is about 4.6 billion years old. The oldest rock is about 3.8 billion years old. Scientists have also dated meteorites that have fallen from space, and must have formed at the same time as the Earth.

WHY DOES THE EARTH SPIN?

The Earth spins because it is falling around the Sun. As the Earth hurtles round the Sun, the Sun's gravity keeps it spinning, just as the Earth's gravity keeps a ball rolling downhill.

EARTH'S ORBIT ROUND THE SUN

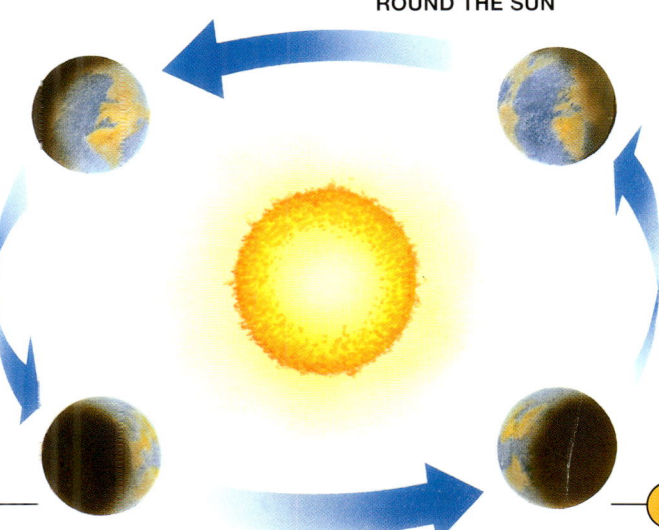

As the Earth orbits the Sun, the hemisphere of the planet that faces the Sun has its summer. The hemisphere facing away is in winter.

WHAT IS THE MOON?

The Moon is the Earth's natural satellite and has circled around it for at least four billion years. It is a rocky ball about a quarter of Earth's size and is held in its orbit by mutual gravitational attraction. Scientists believe that the Moon formed when early in Earth's history a planet smashed into it. The impact was so tremendous that nothing was left of the planet but a few hot splashes thrown back up into space. Within a day of the smash, these splashes had been drawn together by gravity to form the Moon.

THE MOON'S PHASES

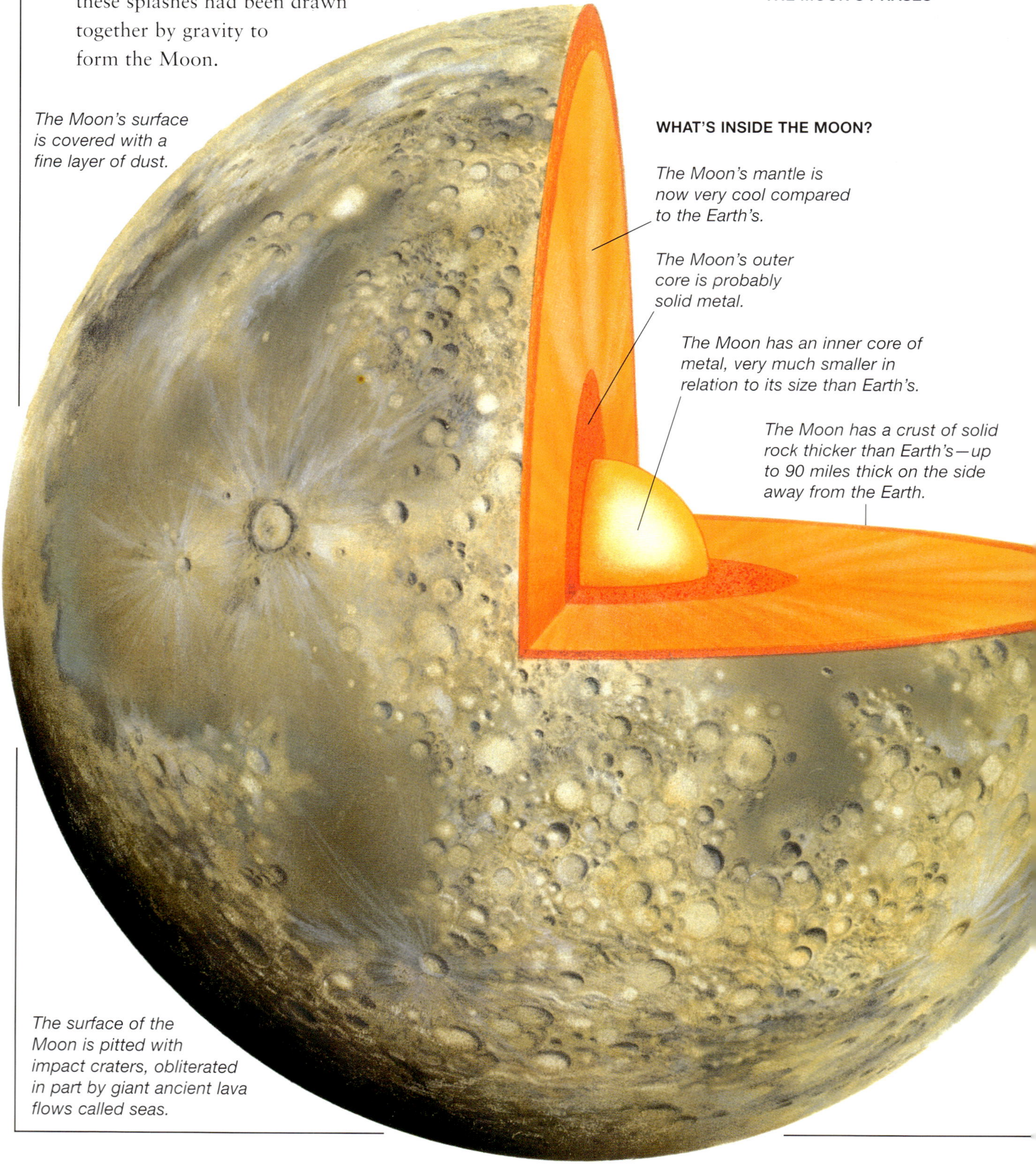

The Moon's surface is covered with a fine layer of dust.

WHAT'S INSIDE THE MOON?

The Moon's mantle is now very cool compared to the Earth's.

The Moon's outer core is probably solid metal.

The Moon has an inner core of metal, very much smaller in relation to its size than Earth's.

The Moon has a crust of solid rock thicker than Earth's—up to 90 miles thick on the side away from the Earth.

The surface of the Moon is pitted with impact craters, obliterated in part by giant ancient lava flows called seas.

WHAT IS A NEW MOON?

The Moon appears to change shape during the month because, as it circles the Earth, we see its bright, sunny side from a different angle. At the new moon, the Moon is between Earth and the Sun, and we catch only a crescent-shaped glimpse of its bright side. Over the first two weeks of the month, we see more and more of the bright side (waxing) until full moon, when we see all its sunny side. Over the next two weeks, we see less and less (waning), until we get back to just a sliver—the old moon.

The phases of the Moon, from left to right: new moon, half moon (waxing), gibbous moon (waxing), full moon, gibbous moon (waning), half moon (waning), old moon.

WHY DOES THE SEA HAVE TIDES?

The Moon's gravity draws the oceans into an oval around the Earth, creating a bulge of water on each side of the world. These bulges stay beneath the Moon as the Earth spins round and so seem to run around the world, making the tide rise and fall as they pass.

WHAT IS A LUNAR ECLIPSE?

As the Moon goes round the Earth, sometimes it passes right into Earth's shadow, where sunlight is blocked off. This is a lunar eclipse. If you look at the Moon during this time, you can see the dark disc of the Earth's shadow creeping across the Moon.

WHAT IS A HARVEST MOON?

The harvest moon is the full moon nearest the September equinox (when night and day are of equal length). This moon hangs above the eastern horizon for several evenings, providing a good light for harvesters.

HOW LONG IS A MONTH?

It takes the Moon 27.3 days to circle the Earth, but 29.53 days from one full moon to the next, because the Earth moves as well. A lunar month is the 29.53 days cycle. Calendar months are entirely artificial.

LUNAR MODULE

WHAT IS MOONLIGHT?

Moonlight is simply the Sun's light reflected off the white dust on the Moon's surface.

WHO WERE THE FIRST MEN ON THE MOON?

The first men on the Moon were Neil Armstrong and Buzz Aldrin of the US Apollo 11 mission who landed on the Moon on July 21, 1969. (As Armstrong set foot on the Moon, he said: "This a small step for a man, a giant leap for mankind.")

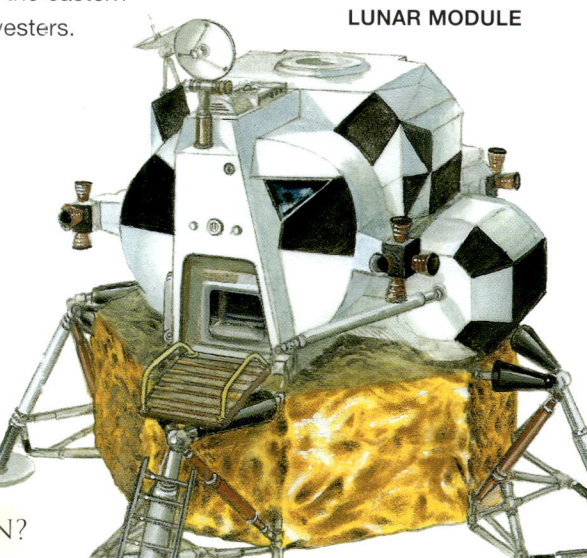

The lunar module from the Apollo 15 mission was the astronauts' home during their brief stay on the Moon.

WHAT IS THE SUN?

The Sun is an average star, just like countless others in the universe. It formed from gas left behind after an earlier, much larger star blew up and now, in middle-age, burns yellow and fairly steadily—giving the Earth daylight and remarkably constant temperatures. Besides heat and light, the Sun sends out deadly gamma rays, X-rays, and ultraviolet, as well as infrared and radio waves. Fortunately we are shielded from these by Earth's magnetic field and atmosphere.

HOW BIG IS THE SUN?

The Sun is a small to medium-sized star 0.86 million miles in diameter. It weighs just under 2,000 trillion trillion tons.

The photosphere is a sea of boiling gas. It gives the heat and light we experience on Earth.

Sunspot

HOW HOT IS THE SUN?

The surface of the Sun is a phenomenal 11,000°F, and would melt absolutely anything. But its core is thousands of times hotter at over 29 million°F!

WHAT ARE SUNSPOTS?

Sunspots are dark blotches seen on the Sun's surface. They are thousands of miles across, and usually occur in pairs. They are dark because they are slightly less hot than the rest of the surface. As the Sun rotates, they slowly cross its face—in about 37 days at the Equator and 26 days at the Poles. The average number of spots seems to reach a maximum every 11 years, and many scientists believe these sunspot maximums are linked to periods of stormier weather on Earth.

WHAT MAKES THE SUN BURN?

The Sun gets its heat from nuclear fusion. Huge pressures deep inside the Sun force the nuclei (cores) of hydrogen atoms to fuse together to make helium atoms, releasing huge amounts of nuclear energy.

Beyond the chromosphere is the sun's ultra-thin halo of boiled-off gases called the corona.

Higher above the chromosphere are giant tongues of hot gases called prominences.

HOW OLD IS THE SUN?

The Sun is a middle-aged star and probably formed about five billion years ago. It will probably burn for another five billion years and then die in a blaze so bright that the Earth will be scorched right out of existence.

WHAT IS A SOLAR ECLIPSE?

A solar eclipse is when the Moon comes in between the Sun and the Earth, creating a shadow a few hundred miles wide on the Earth.

WHAT ARE SOLAR FLARES?

Flares are eruptions from the Sun's surface that fountain into space with the energy of one million atom bombs for about five minutes. (They are similar to solar prominences, the giant flame-like tongues of hot hydrogen that loop 60,000 miles into space.)

The chromosphere is a tenuous layer through which dart tongues called spicules, making it look like a flaming forest.

WHAT ARE THE INNER PLANETS?

The inner planets are the four planets in the solar system that are nearest to the Sun. These planets—Mercury, Venus, Earth, and Mars—are small planets made of rock, unlike the bigger planets further out, which are made mostly of gas. Because they are made of rock, they have a hard surface a spaceship could land on, which is why they are sometimes called terrestrial (earth) planets. They all have a thin atmosphere, but each is very different.

WHAT ARE THE INNER PLANETS MADE OF?

Each of the inner planets is formed a little bit like an egg—with a hard "shell" or crust of rock, a "white" or mantle of soft, semi-molten rock, and a "yolk" or core of hot often molten iron and nickel.

MARS

EARTH

VENUS

Mars is reddish with shadows visible here and there on the surface of the planet.

Three quarters of Earth's surface is covered in water, which is why it looks blue.

Venus is a soft pinkish white ball with no features visible on the surface through its thick atmosphere.

Mercury has virtually no atmosphere and its surface is pitted with craters like the Moon.

MERCURY

WHY IS MARS RED?

Mars is red because it is rusty. The surface contains a high proportion of iron dust, and this has been oxidized in the carbon dioxide atmosphere.

HOW HOT IS MERCURY?

Temperatures on Mercury veer from one extreme to the other because it has too thin an atmosphere to insulate it. In the day, temperatures soar to 800°F; at night they plunge to −290°F.

IS THERE LIFE ON MARS?

The Viking landers of the 1970s found not even the minutest trace of life. But in 1996, microscopic fossils of what might be mini-viruses were found in a rock from Mars. So who knows?

WHAT IS THE AIR ON VENUS?

Venus's atmosphere would be deadly for humans. It is very deep, so the pressure on the ground is huge. It is made mainly of poisonous carbon dioxide and is also filled with clouds of sulphuric acid.

SUN

HOW BIG IS JUPITER?

Very big. Even though Jupiter is largely gas it weighs 320 times as much as the Earth and is 88,850 miles in diameter.

Jupiter has a ring system, like Saturn, but much, much smaller.

SATURN

Saturn's rings are made of billions of tiny chips of dust and ice.

HOW HEAVY IS SATURN?

Saturn may be big, but because it is made largely of liquid hydrogen, it is also remarkably light, with a mass of 600 billion trillion tons. If you could find a big enough bath, it would float.

Winds roar around Saturn's equator at 1,120 mph.

When it rains on Saturn, it rains drops of liquid helium.

WHAT ARE THE GIANT PLANETS?

Jupiter and Saturn—the fifth and sixth planets out from the Sun—are the giants of the solar system. Jupiter is twice as heavy as all the planets put together, and 1,300 times as big as the Earth. Saturn is almost as big. Unlike the inner planets, they are both made largely of gas, and only their very core is rocky. This does not mean they are vast cloud balls. The enormous pressure of gravity means the gas is squeezed until it becomes liquid and even solid.

WHAT ARE SATURN'S RINGS?

Saturn's rings are the planet's shining halo. They are made of countless billions of tiny chips of ice and dust—few bigger than a refrigerator and most the size of ice cubes.

WHAT IS JUPITER'S RED SPOT?

The Great Red Spot or GRS is a huge swirling storm in Jupiter's atmosphere 25,000 miles across that has gone on in the same place for at least 330 years.

Uranus rolls on its side and is the seventh planet out from the Sun.

Neptune is so far from the Sun that surface temperatures drop to –346°F.

URANUS

WHY IS NEPTUNE GREEN?

Neptune is greeny blue because its surface is completely covered in immensely deep oceans of liquid methane (natural gas).

WHAT ARE THE OUTER PLANETS?

The outer planets are Uranus, Neptune, and Pluto, and Pluto's companion Charon. Unlike the other planets, these were completely unknown to ancient astronomers. They are so far away, and so faint, that Uranus was discovered only in 1781, Neptune in 1846, Pluto in 1930, and Charon as recently as 1978. Uranus and Neptune are gas giants like Jupiter and Saturn, but Pluto and Charon are rocky and were probably wandering asteroids trapped by the Sun's gravity within the outer reaches of the solar system.

WHAT IS A METEORITE?

Meteorites are lumps of rock from space big enough to penetrate the Earth's atmosphere and reach the ground without burning up.

At the heart of a comet is a nucleus of ice and dust often shaped like a lumpy potato, just a few miles across.

WHAT'S A COMET?

Spectacular comets are just dirty iceballs a few miles across. Normally, they circle the outer reaches of the solar system. But occasionally, one of them is drawn in toward the Sun. As it hurtles toward the Sun, it melts and a vast tail of gas is blown behind it by the solar wind. We may see this spectacular tail in the night sky shining in the sunlight for a few weeks until it swings round the Sun and out of sight. The most recent comet was Hale-Bopp in 1997.

PLUTO AND CHARON

NEPTUNE

HOW BIG IS PLUTO?

Pluto is very small, which is why it was so hard to spot. It is five times smaller than the Earth—just 1,419 miles across—and 500 times lighter.

WHAT'S AN ASTEROID?

Asteroids are the thousands of rocky lumps that circle round the Sun in a big band between Mars and Jupiter. The biggest, Ceres, is 600 miles across. Most are much smaller. Over 3,200 asteroids have been identified so far.

A COMET IN THE NIGHT SKY

HOW LONG IS A YEAR ON NEPTUNE?

Neptune is so far from the Sun—over 2,800 million miles at maximum—that its orbit takes 164.79 years. So Neptune's year is 164.79 of ours.

A tail of ionized atoms is blown out millions of miles behind the comet by the solar wind.

WHAT IS A LIGHT-YEAR?

A light-year is around 5.88 trillion miles. This is the distance light can travel in a year, at its constant rate of 186,411 miles per second.

HOW DO ASTRONOMERS MEASURE DISTANCE?

For nearby stars, they use parallax (see *What is a parsec?*). With middle distance stars, they look for standard candles, stars whose brightness they know. The dimmer it looks, compared to how bright it should look, the further away it is.

Distances within the solar system can be given in kilometers or miles.

WHAT IS A PARSEC?

A parsec is 3.26 light-years. Parsecs are parallax distances—distances worked out geometrically from slight shifts of a star's apparent position as the Earth moves round the Sun.

WHAT IS THE FURTHEST STAR WE CAN SEE?

The furthest objects we can see in space are quasars, which may be over 13 billion light-years away.

Distances to nearby stars are measured in light-years.

Distances to the furthest galaxies are measured in billions of light-years.

HOW FAR IS IT TO THE NEAREST STAR?

The nearest star is Proxima Centauri, which is 4.3 light-years 25 trillion miles.

WHAT IS RED SHIFT?

When a galaxy is moving rapidly away from us the waves of light become stretched out—that is, they become redder. The greater this red shift, the faster the galaxy is moving away from us.

ARE THE STARS GETTING FURTHER AWAY?

Analysis of red shifts has shown us that every single galaxy is moving away from us. The further away the galaxy, the faster it is moving away from us. The most distant galaxies are receding at almost the speed of light.

HOW FAR AWAY IS THE SUN?

The distance varies between 91 to 94 million miles from Earth. This is measured very accurately by bouncing radar waves off the planets.

HOW FAR AWAY IS THE MOON?

At its nearest, the Moon is 221,463 miles away from Earth; at its furthest, it is 252,710 miles away. This is measured accurately by a laser beam bounced off mirrors left on the Moon's surface by Apollo astronauts and Soviet lunar probes. The distance is shown by how long it takes the beam to travel to the Moon and back.

HOW DID ASTRONOMERS FIRST ESTIMATE THE SUN'S DISTANCE?

In 1672, two astronomers, Cassini in France and Richer in Guiana, noted the exact position of Mars in the skies. They could work out how far away Mars is from the slight difference between their two measurements. Once they knew this, they could work out by simple geometry the distance from Earth to the Sun. Cassini's estimate was a mere 7 percent too low.

OBSERVATORY

The dome rotates, so the telescope can track stars across the sky.

HOW MANY GALAXIES ARE THERE?

With the largest telescopes and most sensitive detectors, we could probably record about a billion galaxies—there may be many, many more beyond their limits.

WHAT ARE DOUBLE STARS?

Our Sun is alone in space, but many stars have one or more nearby companions. Double stars are called binaries.

WHERE IS THE EARTH?

The Earth is just over half way out along one of the spiral arms of the Galaxy, about 30,000 light-years from the center.

The Galaxy is whirling rapidly, sweeping the Sun and the other stars round at 60 billion mph.

WHAT IS A GALAXY?

If we could see the Milky Way from above, we would see that it is a giant spiral galaxy.

Our Sun is just one of a massive collection of two billion stars arranged in a shape like a fried egg, 100,000 light-years across. This collection is called the Galaxy because we see it in the band of stars across the night sky called the Milky Way. (Galaxy comes from the Greek for milky.) But earlier this century it was realized that the Galaxy is just one of millions of similar giant star groups scattered throughout space, which we also call galaxies. The nearest is the Andromeda galaxy.

WHAT IS THE BIGGEST THING IN THE UNIVERSE?

The biggest structure in the universe is the Great Wall—a great sheet of galaxies 500 million light-years long and 16 million light-years thick.

Spiral galaxies are spinning Catherine wheel spirals like our Milky Way.

Elliptical galaxies are shaped like footballs and are the oldest galaxies of all.

SPIRAL GALAXY

ELLIPTICAL GALAXY

The Milky Way is over 100,000 light-years across, 1,000 light-years thick, and contains more than 100 billion stars.

THE MILKY WAY

WHAT IS THE MILKY WAY?

The Milky Way is a pale blotchy white band that stretches right across the night sky. A powerful telescope shows it is made of thousands of stars, and is actually an edge-on view of our Galaxy.

WHAT EXACTLY ARE NEBULAE?

Nebulae are giant clouds of gas and dust spread throughout the galaxies. Some of them we see through telescopes because they shine faintly as they reflect starlight. With others, called dark nebulae, we see only inky black patches hiding the stars behind. This is where stars are born. A few—called glowing nebulae—glow faintly of their own accord as the gas within them is heated by nearby stars.

Irregular galaxies are galaxies that have no particular shape at all.

Arms trail from this type of galaxy like water from a spinning garden sprinkler.

BARRED SPIRAL GALAXY

IRREGULAR GALAXY

A SPACECRAFT ORBITING EARTH

The craft shoots off into space if its forward momentum exceeds the acceleration due to Earth's gravity.

WHAT DID NEWTON DISCOVER?

The discoveries of Isaac Newton (1642-1727) include the three fundamental laws of motion. He also discovered the force called gravity, which holds the Moon in orbit around the Earth, and the planets in orbit around the Sun.

HOW STRONG IS A PLANET'S GRAVITY?

The more massive the planet—that is the more matter it contains—the more powerful its gravity. Astronauts on the Moon could jump up high in heavy spacesuits, because the Moon is much smaller than the Earth and its gravity is weaker.

A craft orbiting Earth is effectively falling around it, pulled by the Earth's gravity.

WHAT IS GRAVITY?

Gravity is the mutual attraction between every single bit of matter in the universe. The more matter there is, and the closer it is, the stronger the attraction. A big dense planet pulls much more than a small one, or one that is far away. The Sun is so big, it makes its pull felt over millions of miles of space. The Earth is smaller, but big enough to keep the Moon circling around it. The weight of an object is simply how hard gravity is pulling on it.

The black hole contains so much matter in such a small space that its gravitational pull even drags in light.

WHAT IS A BLACK HOLE?

If a small star is very dense, it may begin to shrink under the pull of its own gravity. As it shrinks, it becomes denser and denser and its gravity becomes more and more powerful—until it shrinks to a single tiny point of infinite density called singularity. The gravitational pull of a singularity is so immense that it pulls space into a "hole" like a funnel. This is the black hole, which sucks in everything that comes near it with its huge gravitational force—including light, which is why it is a "black" hole.

A giant black hole may exist at the center of our galaxy.

We may be able to spot a black hole from the powerful radio signals emitted by stars being ripped to shreds as they are sucked in.

HOW BIG IS A BLACK HOLE?

The singularity at the heart of a black hole is infinitely small. The size of the hole around it depends on how much matter went into forming it. The black hole at the heart of our galaxy may be around the size of the solar system.

WHAT HAPPENS INSIDE A BLACK HOLE?

Nothing that goes into a black hole comes out, and there is a point of no return called the event horizon. If you went beyond this you would be "spaghettified"—stretched long and thin until you were torn apart by the immense gravity.

165

QUIZ
QUESTIONS

SECTION ONE

OUR
PLANET

1 What are the three main eras of earth's history called?

2 What is lava?

3 What are the structures that hang down from the ceilings of caves called?

4 What are deltas?

5 Where are the largest ice sheets found?

6 What is the name of the dry waterways found in deserts?

7 What is the name of an ice sheet that juts out into the sea?

8 What is the longest river in the world?

OUR BODY

1   What is the point where two bones meet called?

2   Can muscles push as well as pull?

3   Why do we need to sleep?

4   Why do we need to blink?

5   How do we measure sound?

6   Which area of the tongue is sensitive to sweet tastes?

7   What is the color of blood that is rich in oxygen?

8   What is the name of the organ that feeds the unborn baby?

SECTION THREE

LOOKING BACK

1   When did primates first appear on earth?

2   What did Egyptians use to protect their grain stores?

3   Who were believed to be the best soldiers in Ancient Greece?

4   What was Hadrian's Wall designed to do?

5   What was the name of the Inca sun god?

6   Who were the samurai?

7   When was the first railroad opened?

8   Who launched the first space satellite?

SECTION FOUR
COUNTRIES AND THEIR PEOPLES

1 Which is the biggest continent?

2 Which is the world's smallest nation?

3 What is the name for people who have no fixed home, but move from one place to another?

4 Which famous building looks like a sailing boat?

5 How does a hovercraft work?

6 What are the best conditions for growing rice?

7 What is the name of the Hindu festival of light?

8 Where is the oldest theater?

1 What are the horizontal arms on a crane called?

2 Who designed the first water closet?

3 What is an ultrasound scanner often used for?

4 What did the US Defense Department's ARPAnet project lead to?

5 When were personal stereos first introduced?

6 What is a Manned Maneuvering Unit used for?

7 Who sketched the first idea for a tank?

8 What machine will help surgeons to perform operations in the future?

SECTION FIVE
MAGNIFICENT MACHINES

PLANT LIFE

1 What is the name of the process green plants use to make their food?

2 Why have many flowers evolved colors and scent to attract animals?

3 How do algae help to clean up sewage?

4 What is the name of the largest cactus?

5 Why do some mountain plants reproduce without flowers?

6 What is the name given to soil that is permanently frozen?

7 What is the most important food to come from the wetlands?

8 Which plants are used to make sugar?

SECTION SEVEN

EVERY LIVING CREATURE

1 Which is the smallest rodent?

2 Where do leopards live?

3 Does a giraffe have more bones in its neck than any other mammal?

4 How big are the family groups of the chimpanzees?

5 Which is the biggest baby in the animal kingdom?

6 Which is the fiercest freshwater fish?

7 Which is the world's most dangerous snake?

8 Which is the biggest bird of prey?

SECTION EIGHT

HOW DOES IT WORK?

1   What are the three states of matter?

2   What is a molecule?

3   What did Marie Curie discover?

4   Where and when was the first atomic bomb invented?

5   What is the name given to the double spiral molecule that is found inside every living cell?

6   What is the name given to the force of attraction between every bit of matter in the Universe?

7   How are rainbows formed?

8   How far does the Earth's magnetic field extend?

SECTION NINE

OUT IN SPACE

1   What are the two things needed to support life on a planet?

2   When did men first land on the Moon?

3   What is the name of the shadow cast on the Earth when the Moon comes between the Sun and the Earth?

4   Which are the inner planets?

5   What is a meteorite?

6   What is the name of the nearest star?

7   What is the name of an area in space which sucks everything into itself, even light?

8   What is the name of the nearest galaxy to ours?

QUIZ
ANSWERS

OUR PLANET
1   Paleozoic, Mesozoic, and Cenozoic
2   Molten rock
3   Stalactites
4   Areas of sediments that pile up around the mouths of some rivers
5   In Antarctica and Greenland
6   Wadis
7   Ice shelf
8   The Nile

OUR BODY
1   A joint
2   No
3   To rest our muscles and allow the body time to repair damaged cells
4   To clean and protect the eye
5   In decibels
6   The tip
7   Bright red
8   Placenta

LOOKING BACK
1   About 50 million years ago
2   Cats
3   Spartans
4   To guard the frontiers of the Roman Empire against attacks from the Celts
5   Inti
6   Japanese warriors
7   1825
8   Russia

COUNTRIES AND THEIR PEOPLES
1   Asia
2   Vatican City
3   Nomads
4   The Sydney Opera House
5   It floats on a cushion of air
6   Flooded fields (paddies)
7   Diwali
8   Vicenza, Italy

MAGNIFICENT MACHINES
1   Jibs
2   Sir John Hartington (Elizabeth I's godson)
3   To look at an unborn baby
4   The worldwide network or Internet

5   In 1979
6   It is used by astronauts to walk in zero gravity
7   Leonardo da Vinci
8   Virtual reality machine

PLANT LIFE
1   Photosynthesis
2   So that they will help with pollination
3   They feed on the pollutants in the water and help to make it clean
4   Giant cactus or saguaro
5   Because there are so few insects to pollinate them
6   Permafrost
7   Rice
8   Sugar cane and sugar beet

EVERY LIVING CREATURE
1   The pygmy mouse
2   In Africa and Asia
3   No
4   Between 25 and 100 animals
5   A baby whale
6   The piranha
7   The saw-scaled carpet viper
8   The Andean condor

HOW DOES IT WORK?
1   Solid, liquid, and gas
2   The smallest particle of a substance that can exist on its own
3   The elements polonium and radium
4   In the USA toward the end of the Second World War
5   DNA (deoxyribonucleic acid)
6   Gravity
7   By the reflection of the Sun off billions of drops of moisture in the air
8   50,000 miles

OUT IN SPACE
1   Water and oxygen
2   July 1969
3   Solar eclipse
4   Mercury, Venus, Earth, and Mars
5   A lump of rock from space
6   Proxima Centauri
7   A black hole
8   Andromeda Galaxy

INDEX